Vicarious trauma in the legal profession

Joanna Fleck is a consultant, teacher and writer working across a range of projects at the intersection of mental health, physical health and social justice. She runs reflective practice groups and community mental health projects for a local Mind in London. She teaches trauma-informed yoga and mindfulness and is undertaking training in psychotherapy and counselling. She has an MSc in Psychology with research on secondary traumatic stress in the legal profession. This research and ongoing study informs the work of Claiming Space. Until 2019 she was also a solicitor practicing in civil liberties and inquests.

Rachel Francis is a barrister at One Pump Court Chambers, called to the Bar in 2012. She practises in immigration and family law, with particular expertise in the overlap between these two areas of law and in working with exceptionally vulnerable clients. She is the former co-chair of Young Legal Aid Lawyers (YLAL). During her time as co-chair of YLAL, Rachel saw first-hand the effects of working with trauma in the legal profession. She was jointly responsible for the strategic direction of YLAL, for co-ordinating its campaigning work, and for promoting social mobility and protecting the interests of junior lawyers who believe in the importance of legal-aided work as a means of achieving social justice. In July 2019 Rachel was awarded the LAPG Special Award for outstanding commitment to access to justice. She is a regular speaker at legal conferences and in legal publications on trauma-informed working practices and the collective need for self-care. She featured on the BBC Radio 4 programme *Seriously...Barristers on the Brink* with Afua Hirsh, speaking about the mental health crisis at the Bar.

Together they founded *Claiming Space*, a social enterprise that provides training, consultancy and peer support services. Joanna and Rachel met whilst on the committee of YLAL. Following many conversations with peers and colleagues about the impact of client stories on individual and collective wellbeing, they began to develop a project to make space to learn, share, and reflect on our practice and its impact. Out of these conversations, Claiming Space was formed. It is the product of Joanna and Rachel's years of working in legal aid and speaking to lawyers from across the spectrum of social justice legal practice. The ultimate goal of Claiming Space is to ensure that the most vulnerable in society are helped by lawyers who are well-supported to deal with stress, vicarious trauma, and burnout.

The Legal Action Group is a national, independent charity which campaigns for equal access to justice for all members of society.
Legal Action Group:

- provides support to the practice of lawyers and advisers
- inspires developments in that practice
- campaigns for improvements in the law and the administration of justice
- stimulates debate on how services should be delivered.

Vicarious trauma in the legal profession

a practical guide to trauma, burnout and collective care

Joanna Fleck and Rachel Francis

 Legal Action Group
2021

This edition published in Great Britain 2021
by LAG Education and Service Trust Limited
c/o Oliver Fisher Solicitors, Royalty Studios
105–109 Lancaster Road
London W11 1QF
www.lag.org.uk

British Library Cataloguing in Publication Data

a CIP catalogue record for this book is available from the British Library.

This book has been produced using Forest Stewardship
Council (FSC) certified paper. The wood used to produce
FSC certified products with a 'Mixed Sources' label comes
from FSC certified well-managed forests, controlled sources
and/or recycled material

print ISBN 978 1 913648 10 7
ebook ISBN 978 1 913648 11 4
print / ebook bundle ISBN 978 1 913648 12 1

Typeset by Refinecatch Ltd, Bungay, Suffolk
Printed in Great Britain by Hobbs the Printers, Totton, Hampshire

Caring for myself is not self-indulgence, it is self-preservation, and that is an act of political warfare.

Audre Lorde, A Burst of Light: And Other Essays[1]

---

1 *A Burst of Light: And Other Essays*, p130, Courier Dover Publications, 13 September 2017.

Foreword

by Baroness Helena Kennedy QC

Content warning: traumatic case detail

Some years ago, I was giving a lecture about domestic abuse and the catalogue of cases I had done defending women who had killed their abusive partners after years of vicious assaults and coercive behaviour. Homicide against a backdrop of violence had become my daily round. I had also done many cases involving cruelty to children as well as cases involving terrorist bombings, or asylum-seekers who had fled persecution and unfathomable torture, including multiple rapes and mutilation. A question came from the audience which I had never been asked before. What does it do to *you*? I gave the answer that I believed then. I said I had been very emotionally affected by the experiences of my clients, particularly when I was young, but practice over many years meant I found a way of keeping those emotions contained, while still retaining the empathy that I felt was essential to good representation.

I reflected on that answer often in the years thereafter as my work became more international, especially a couple of years ago when I went on a United Nations mission to help investigate the killing of Jamal Khashoggi, the journalist who was assassinated in the Saudi Arabian Consulate by a Saudi hit squad and his body dismembered with an electric saw. The grotesque killing was recorded by Turkish Intelligence, who had bugged the premises, and listening to the tapes of Khashoggi's death was the stuff of nightmares. Bad dreams also followed my journey to Iraqi refugee camps to take testimonies from Yazidi women who have been enslaved and multiply raped by ISIS militias. It would be wrong to suggest that our clients' trauma does not stay with us. And sometimes they are haunting. However, my mainly legal aid practice of over 40 years allowed me to live a decent life in a nice home and to afford childcare and regular holidays. My physical and mental wellbeing were taken care of. I felt proud of my work and my professional status. Those were the days!

For lawyers now doing the work I have spent my life doing, the reality is very different. The legal landscape has changed beyond imagining. So I am now asking: what are traumatic cases doing to *them?*

I am now sitting as a member of a Cross Party Parliamentary Inquiry into Legal Aid, looking into the desperate situation in our courts where there is a huge backlog of cases and a legal profession that is on its knees. Why, you may wonder? Aren't legal aid lawyers those 'fat cats' we hear about from politicians and tabloid newspapers, raking in tons of money from the taxpayer to represent the undeserving? Don't you believe it.

Over the last couple of decades legal aid has become a political football with the parties competing to show who could be more swingeing in their cuts. The last 10 years has seen 40 per cent taken out of the Ministry of Justice budget and the most horrifying assault upon access to justice and legal professionalism has ensued; the heart has been torn out of legal aid. The young lawyers who choose to act for the most disadvantaged in society do so as a vocational choice but, even though they have studied and trained for about 5/6 years, they now earn so little they cannot afford a mortgage or a reasonable place to live. They do tragic cases for the most vulnerable of clients. Over and over I hear the accounts of young lawyers working so intensely just to do their best for traumatised clients that they face burnout within a few years: long hours, last minute cases, anxiety about failing their clients because of inadequate time to research and prepare, and an inability to make a decent living or afford a family. And into that mix goes the pain of their clients which is ingested and taken home.

I felt very privileged to be asked to write the foreword to this special book. I think it should be used to help lawyers (and their employers or professional organisations) recognise that it is not surprising they feel anxious and stressed out. We have created a society which does not value the things that matter. Austerity policies saw public services decimated. As public service lawyers, we have to look after ourselves in order to do our job well and to find satisfaction in it; that is hard in a system being so profoundly damaged because it is starved of funds. Acting as lawyers for people at extreme moments in their lives – facing eviction, conviction, loss of liberty, deportation, loss of their children, the end of a marriage, sexual or domestic violence, detention in mental facilities – places a great burden on our shoulders. We are conducting their cases, arguing on their behalf, and the outcome may change their lives forever.

No professional person should be unsupported in their work nor so poorly rewarded that their survival in the profession they love is put at risk. This book is a wake-up call about what is happening to law and access to justice – but it is also a clarion as to what is happening to lawyers.

Baroness Helena Kennedy QC
January 2021

Preface

In early 2017 we started to discuss how we could work together to support the wellbeing of fellow junior lawyers. We knew that other organisations and individuals were already doing vital work but were both certain that there was more urgent work to do. What we did not know was how pervasive the issue might be or how willing people might be to talk about it. We had both experienced and seen in our peers and colleagues the damaging negative effects of working with trauma, even if we didn't always have the vocabulary to describe it.

Since we created Claiming Space in 2017, there has been a slow and steady growth in interest and research into vicarious trauma in the legal profession and our understanding of the depth of the issue has grown. Over the last three years, we have learnt from academic study, personal research, from other professionals working with trauma and, most importantly, through talking to lawyers across the country.

This work, and this book, comes in the context of a boom in what might be called 'mental health awareness'. In the legal profession more broadly, there is a growing focus on wellbeing and stress. Although this change is welcomed, those of us working in the social justice sector are often cynical about 'progress' that reinforces a neoliberal agenda, transferring the burden to the individual to become more 'resilient'. Through our work together and with other organisations we know that there is a great appetite for resources and spaces that move beyond this limiting view of mental health and wellbeing.

At the same time, the rapid change in how news is circulated and consumed has increased our exposure to injustice and trauma outside of our caseloads. With the growth of the Black Lives Matter movement there has been a greater understanding of the impact on Black people being regularly exposed to racist policing not just directly but vicariously through traditional and social media.

The rise of nationalism across the globe and the climate emergency leave us in no doubt that the fight for the rights of the vulnerable and of migrants and racialised groups will be a long and a hard one. The added pressures from a global pandemic have exacerbated the systemic inequities affecting our clients and have in many cases worsened the experience of lawyers on the frontline, particularly at the junior end.

There can be no doubt that substantive practical support is needed for all of those working to protect and enforce the rights of the individual against the state.

Through our work over the last few years we know that there is a great deal of effort and care being taken across the profession. Unfortunately there remains a level of ignorance and scepticism about the severity or importance of the issue of vicarious trauma. This can be particularly pernicious when it exists at the senior end of the profession, with junior and senior staff alike made to feel that they do not really belong in the profession if they are experiencing the more difficult effects of vicarious trauma.

Whilst it is beyond the scope and research of this book to examine in depth the many ways in which trauma intersects with class, race and discrimination – and acknowledging both authors hold privilege on many levels in this regard – we hope that it is clear throughout that these are real and live issues that must be addressed in any consideration of vicarious trauma and burnout.

About this book

The first half sets out the theory and research into trauma, burnout and self-care, both in the legal profession and more broadly. This information will hopefully be a useful resource for those seeking to make the argument for change in their own organisations or across the professions.

The second half moves from theory to practice, examining how we might take action at an individual, team, and profession-wide level. In doing so we acknowledge the steps that are already being taken by individuals and organisations to put theory into practice.

Throughout we draw on real-life case studies from lawyers in their own words. We also offer suggestions for ways to pause and reflect as you read the book.

While we use the term 'lawyer' throughout this book, that term is used generically and intended to capture, caseworkers, legal executives and other legal practitioners. This book applies, and is relevant, to all of those practitioners, and may strike a cord with those working in other similar roles, including in non-legal settings.

This book is not intended to provide answers to all of the challenges we face in dealing with vicarious trauma. We hope instead that it helps to point practitioners in the right direction and to provide a practical tool for self-reflection and action.

Let's get to work.

Joanna Fleck
Rachel Francis
January 2021

Acknowledgements

We would like to thank the extraordinary and courageous lawyers who have spoken with us anonymously about their experiences of stress, burnout, and vicarious trauma for this book. We are also extremely grateful for all of those lawyers whom we have met since September 2017 when we began our work as co-directors of Claiming Space. This book would not have been written without the honesty, candour and brilliance of all of these lawyers. Nor would it have been written without the courage and strength of our clients, past, present, and future, who provide inspiration and drive to practitioners on a daily basis: thank you to all of our clients.

We would like to thank those who have supported and championed Claiming Space, from the time that it was an idea without a name, right up to the present moment. Your support has been invaluable.

We owe great thanks to everyone who has supported us during the process of writing this book: our publisher, our readers, and those many, wonderful, unnamed people behind the scenes. We are indebted to you all.

Lawyers who work in legal aid and social welfare law, championing the rights and needs of their clients, are our inspiration and our drive. It is for them that this book is written.

Contents

About this book

Grounding practices

One of the core messages of this book is the importance of developing practices, strategies and profession-wide structures that allow space and time for reflection.

Practising mindfulness or grounding techniques can support us when our mind and body are experiencing a difficult stress response. They are also important practices to develop to allow us to pay attention to how and when our work affects us.

We invite you to take pauses throughout the book to see how the content lands, and to take pauses when you need.

These practices are not about trying to *feel better* – but to get *better at feeling.*

We can start this process with ourselves, right now, as we read this book:

1) Bringing your attention to your posture, your feet on the floor, your hands, the muscles in your face. What can you notice? For example, there may be feeling of tension, tingling, blankness, warmth, coolness.
2) Maybe there is a lot of vivid sensation in your body, maybe things are a bit numb today, or maybe things are somewhere in between.
3) You may wish to close your eyes for a moment (this, like all of the guidance here, is optional).
4) What thoughts, images or stories are arising in your mind? Can you take notice less of the content but of the quality of mind right now – is the mind busy, buzzing, planning, remembering? Or is it a little foggy, disconnected? Or something else entirely?
5) Finally, draw your attention to an anchor in the body for a few moments – you may wish to pay attention to the breath or the soles of your feet on the floor, or elsewhere.

Notes on the text

This book is not intended to provide any therapeutic support, and the authors are not mental health clinicians. It is not intended to be a substitute for proper trauma-informed workplace support, training and supervision.

There are a number of resources outlined at the end of the book. If you recognise that the effects of working in this field are affecting your ability to work or live well, then *do not hesitate* to contact a mental health professional or speak to your GP.

We hope and intend that this book lifts any remaining stigma around the topic of vicarious trauma in the legal profession. It is a call to arms to take all steps necessary to support, train and care for ourselves, so that we are here to advocate for today's clients and those future clients that we have not yet met.

Content warnings

We will not be detailing the specifics of traumatic events in this book. However, we may refer to very brief details (for example, in the case studies of other lawyers). We will provide content warnings – marked 'CW' – to enable you to choose whether to read on.

Abbreviations

ACT	acceptance and commitment therapy
APA	America Psychiatric Association
BPTC	Bar Professional Training Course
BSB	Bar Standards Board
CBT	cognitive behavioural therapy
CILEx	Chartered Institute of Legal Executives
CPD	continuing professional development
CPS	Crown Prosecution Service
CPTSD	complex post-traumatic stress disorder
CW	content warning
DSM	*Diagnostic and statistical manual of mental disorders*
EAP	employee assistance programme
EHRC	Equality and Human Rights Commission
EMDR	eye movement desensitisation and reprocessing
GAS	general adaptation syndrome
HMCTS	HM Courts and Tribunals Service
HR	human resources
ICD	*International classification of diseases*
JLD	Junior Lawyers Division of The Law Society
LAA	Legal Aid Agency
LASPO	Legal Aid, Sentencing and Punishment of Offenders Act 2012
LPC	Legal Practice Course
MBCT	mindfulness-based cognitive therapy
MBSR	mindfulness-based stress reduction
NGO	non-governmental organisation
ProQOL	Professional Quality of Life Scale
PTSD	post-traumatic stress disorder
REL	registered European lawyer
RFL	registered foreign lawyer
SRA	Solicitors Regulation Authority
STS	secondary traumatic stress
TIA	trauma-informed approach
VTS	Vicarious Trauma Scale
WHO	World Health Organization
YLAL	Young Legal Aid Lawyers

PART I

History, context, research and theory

Introduction

It is very tempting to take the side of the perpetrator. All the perpetrator asks is that the bystander do nothing. He appeals to the universal desire to see, hear and speak no evil. The victim, on the contrary, asks the bystander to share the burden of pain. The victim demands action, engagement and remembering.[1]

---

1 Judith Herman, *Trauma and recovery: the aftermath of violence – from domestic abuse to political terror*, 1992, pp7–8.

Context

If you have ever had to explain to your friend or family member that unfortunately, no, you are unable to draft them a contract for their new online business or advise them on their mortgage terms, you've probably found yourself explaining that lawyers – despite being one profession – are made up of discrete areas of expertise.

You might also have explained that it is our professional duty to ensure that we have received the requisite specialist training for our area of expertise, and that we could not ethically advise or practise in an area for which we had not received adequate training.

However, as lawyers working in legal aid, social justice or with survivors of injury, we regularly work with traumatic and emotionally potent caseloads and often draw on skills for which we have had no formal training.

In parallel with a wider societal awareness, there has been a growing conversation within the legal profession about the mental health of lawyers. However, this conversation tends to be dominated by large city firms whose work, while undoubtedly stressful and full of pressure, is at the other end of the spectrum from that of legal aid lawyers. It also tends to describe mental health as a primarily personal issue: the individual's work/life balance; stress as a personal response.

We may face some common challenges: balancing demanding clients with court deadlines; time and billing targets; ethical conflicts; strict professional obligations; and a culture of never switching off – even, frequently, when on holiday or a non-working day. Lawyers in our sector, however, have another layer added: *the traumatic nature of the content of the cases we work on.*

We bear witness to the pain of our clients, to the suffering that humans inflict upon each other, and to the incredible strength of survivors of violence, torture and abuse of all kinds.

On top of this, we deal with the financial pressure of working on legal aid rates, conditional fee agreements or discounted private rates; a relentlessly hostile political environment; limited and over-stretched resources and support; and, particularly in the early stages of the profession, poor rates of pay.

While the impact of trauma is not separate from the other conditions in which we work (and we will examine those in this book), it demands a separate and central focus because of the little attention it has been given thus far.

There is much excellent practice across the profession, and many lawyers will be passing on these skills to incomers to the profession. Individual organisations across the profession have long been working on this issue, some naming it as vicarious trauma (such as Freedom From Torture[2] who have been providing training on the topic for immigration lawyers working with torture survivors for many years) and others working in informal ways, learning from the good practice of colleagues in the legal and mental health professions. More recently, the Law Society of Scotland has introduced specific guidance on trauma-informed working.[3] The mental health charity for the legal profession, LawCare, provides resources on their website.[4] The authors – in their work through Claiming Space – have worked alongside individuals and organisations working to make impactful and long-lasting change in the profession. However, there is certainly much more work to do.

What is vicarious trauma?

Vicarious trauma, at its first level, is a mode of exposure. The term may be used to simply describe the process of being exposed to trauma (in its broadest sense), vicariously, ie not experiencing it directly, but instead:

• witnessing the event in real time;
• witnessing after the event – for example, listening to our clients, reading witness statements or watching CCTV (all commonplace activities in the life of a lawyer);
• being a first responder witnessing the aftermath (possible for lawyers working in police stations or dealing with clients in acute crisis); or
• being in the physical presence of someone who is experiencing post-traumatic stress.

In this meaning of the term, it is clear that vicarious trauma is a live topic for lawyers across a varied spectrum of practices, from criminal defence to family law, immigration, and any area involving vulnerable populations. It is part of lawyers' work in law centres and debt

---

2   See: www.freedomfromtorture.org.
3   'Trauma informed training': www.lawscot.org.uk/members/cpd-training/trauma-informed-training/.
4   'Trauma informed training': https://www.lawcare.org.uk/information-and-support/vicarious-trauma.

advice clinics, in boutique law firms, personal injury and clinical negligence sets, and in the charity sector.

Of course, those lawyers acting on the other side of our cases (usually representing state agents or insurers) will also be exposed to much of this material. Whilst we acknowledge this fact, this book is not aimed at those lawyers – it is a book for *claimant lawyers*, those who find themselves working with traumatised persons and within traumatising systems. However, those working in criminal defence and family law in particular will have experience of acting for (alleged or proven) perpetrators of trauma.

In some areas of the law, exposure to trauma is merely a likely possibility, but in others it is inevitable. Lawyers make decisions on risk all of the time. We should be taking into account the risks associated with vicarious exposure to trauma in our individual and collective planning.

There is a small but growing evidence-base upon which to begin to assess this risk. It is not possible, yet, to statistically calculate the risk of serious negative trauma over the working life of a lawyer. However, the evidence that has been collated across the globe and in the UK sends a terrifying warning call that must be heeded. Lawyers are struggling and suffering right now.

The evidence is explored in more detail below. In summary, a number of studies have found that lawyers working with traumatic material are likely to express higher levels of trauma-related symptoms than lawyers working in other sectors, as well as when compared to other trauma-exposed professions (eg social workers).

However, not every person who is exposed to trauma develops traumatic stress symptoms, nor is the likelihood of developing such symptoms *solely* explained by levels of exposure to it (the volume of caseloads) or the severity of the traumatic material (indeed some research has found no significant link[5]). A number of environmental, organisational and personal factors are also relevant.

It is important to keep in mind that we will each respond in different ways to exposure to distressing and painful aspects of our cases. Some of these responses will negatively impact our quality of life, professionally and personally. We may well also be impacted positively.

---

5 R Ivicic and R Motta (2017) 'Variables associated with secondary stress among mental health professional', *Traumatology*, 23(2), 196-204. http://psycnet.apa.org/doi/10.1037/trm0000065.

However, it is important to acknowledge that these responses are ultimately 'normal' reactions to 'abnormal' events.

A critical component of trauma-informed working is that firms and organisations recognise the multiplicity of responses to the everyday experience of traumatic caseloads and that it is highly likely, if not inevitable, that workers will be impacted.

> 'I think it is incredibly important that firms understand that people have different propensities to stress and burnout and vicarious trauma: acknowledging that it is an individual situation and not just thinking that overall people can cope ... That is not usually the case for people with this type of work. Shifting from this mentality that it is weak to speak out if you are not coping.'
>
> *Solicitor*

What is trauma?

Definitions of 'trauma'

A guide to terms

Trauma – the incident (or series of events, or daily exposure vicariously).

Traumatic stress – the stress response invoked by the trauma.

Post-traumatic stress – an ongoing stress response going beyond the incident and aftermath.

Vicarious trauma – a mode of exposure to a traumatic incident.

Trauma is:

an emotional response to a terrible event[1]

unprocessed dread[2]

Psychological trauma is an affliction of the powerless. At the moment of trauma, the victim is rendered helpless by overwhelming force. The force is that of nature, we speak of disasters. When the force is that of other human beings, we speak of atrocities. Traumatic events overwhelm the ordinary systems of care that give people a sense of control, connection and meaning.[3]

events that are psychologically overwhelming for individuals, families, or communities.[4]

. . . trauma is also a wordless story our body tells itself about what is safe and what is a threat. Our rational brain can't stop it from occurring, and it can't talk our body out of it. Trauma can cause us to react to present events in ways that seem wildly inappropriate, overly charged, or otherwise out of proportion. Whenever someone freaks out suddenly or reacts to a small problem as if it were a catastrophe, it's often a trauma response. Something in the here and now is rekindling old pain or discomfort, and the body tries to address it with the reflexive energy that's still stuck inside the nervous system.[5]

1 APA: www.apa.org/topics/trauma.
2 David J Morris, *The evil hours: a biography of post-traumatic stress disorder*, Houghton Mifflin Harcourt, 2016, p10.
3 Judith Herman, *Trauma and recovery: the aftermath of violence—from domestic abuse to political terror*, 1992, p33.
4 Regel and Joseph, 2017, p6.
5 Menakem.

Each person's trauma response may be the echo of a necessary response an isolated incident or learned responses which were once useful for survival (possibly from childhood or other earlier experiences) which become a more habitual in times of stress. Of course, we have learned or habitual responses that are helpful in the long-term, unhelpful, damaging, or (likely) a mixture.

Practice: finding an anchor

When we engage with emotive or distressing content, it can be easy to lose our connection to ourselves. We might distract ourselves (consciously or not) from how we are feeling.

We might do this by reverting to our usual lawyerly thinking mode – planning, remembering, sorting, analysing. Getting things 'done' rather than acknowledging how things are.

We might feel numb, blank or spacey.

If we are not aware of how our work – including the 'work' of reading this book – affects us, then it is difficult to take the right care of ourselves and implement the right strategies.

One way that we can stay connected with ourselves is by finding an *anchor* in our own body that can connect us to our present moment experience.

One common anchor is the breath, as is traditionally practised in many meditation traditions. However, if we are new to this kind of practice, are feeling anxious or panicked, or for any other reason, paying attention to the breath can be stressful. Other options are to pay attention to the sensations in the feet, hands, the feeling of a comforting object in our hands, or sounds. We can connect back to the present moment through paying attention to these details.

Stress

The work of a lawyer is stressful. Whatever the content of our case-load, we contend with a multitude of stressors, for example:

- billing targets;
- never-ending roll of deadlines;
- constantly 'fire-fighting' problems;
- rules and regulations;
- demanding clients;
- conflict with colleagues;

- difficult judges;
- commuting to the office or travelling to court and police stations.

These can all trigger the stress response of the body.[6] General stress – known as the 'alarm state' – provides our body with the resources to address our immediate environment. We might recognise our own signs of the 'alarm state' which can – in the short-term – give us an increase of focus and energy.

However, when the stress is prolonged, and we do not have any opportunity to rest between stressful situations (which is not uncommon in a busy legal practice), we may enter the 'resistance' state, where we start to draw on our energy reserves and make greater demands on our body's resources, leading to a depletion in our ability to work or function effectively. Over time this response can lead to total exhaustion.

'I have had – particularly in early practice and when the decisions were really significant, so normally a Placement Order application – I'd be making my way to court, and I haven't wanted to arrive to court. I just would have this urge of not wanting to arrive at court . . . I got off the train once, a couple of stops early; I just got off and sat on the platform, and then got on the next train. I think it was the anxiety, or the stress, or the stakes which were at play.'

Barrister

The stress response is designed to respond to immediate stressors, after which the body can return to a state of relative rest. *Chronic* stress can lead to overwhelm, exhaustion, anxiety, depression, burnout and poor physical health and mental wellbeing.

---

6   The 'general adaptation syndrome' (GAS) conceptualised by Hans Selye, a Hungarian Canadian endocrinologist born in the early 20th century who developed the modern medical understanding of stress. GAS describes the three stages of responses that the body goes through after being triggered by a stressor: alarm, resistance and exhaustion.

'I took some time out for health reasons. When I returned I was having to take a lot more care of myself to stay well but the firm wanted the old version of me whilst I was also learning a new area of the law. I think they were disappointed in me. The firm was demanding in other ways and the support, as well as the way they communicated with me, was really unhelpful. I was trying to cope with difficult physical health conditions but they wanted the person who was willing to sacrifice their evenings and weekends, or to at least push myself, which effectively would have sacrificed my health. They wanted me to just be as productive and work as much as I had done before (which were unsustainable levels of work).'

Casework consultant

Trauma

Trauma can be a physical one (a wound or injury). It can also be a psychological one: a 'wounding' of one's sense of safety, dignity or belonging.

A traumatic event is generally considered to be one in which we experience a threat to our life, bodily integrity or sense of safety. *Traumatic stress* is the stress response reaction to that event, or series of events. *Stress responses* – including those to traumatic events – are adaptive responses, in that they are designed to aide our survival under threat. A *post-traumatic stress response* is one where the response outlasts the threat, causing longer-term dysregulation of the threat-perception system. We can therefore understand traumatic stress responses as normal, adaptive reactions to shocking and abnormal events.

This book intentionally focusses on *vicarious trauma*, but we recognise that *non-traumatic* stress responses and *traumatic* stress responses are expressions along a sliding scale. There is a wide grey area in the middle, but the two extremes are significantly different. There is evidence of a difference at a physiological level in stress hormone release between non-traumatic ('controllable') stressors and traumatic stressors.[7] Anecdotally, from our experience, lawyers

7 GE Miller, E Chen and ES Zhou. 'If it goes up, must it come down? Chronic stress and the hypothalamic-pituitary-adrenocortical axis in humans', *Psychological Bulletin*, (2007) 133(1), 25–45. https://doi.org/10.1037/0033-2909.133.1.25.

recognise that there is a difference between the stress that they experience compared to that experienced by colleagues and friends working in, for example, corporate law.

Lawyers or caseworkers who do not regularly work with trauma but who have experience of traumatic events outside of work, or do so only occasionally, may find the resources in this book useful.

Research into traumatic stress finds 'positive' responses in people who have not been exposed to the particular traumatic event that is the subject of the research. In a recent Canadian study that compared lawyers who are exposed to trauma in their caseload with lawyers who were not, it was found that 6.5 per cent of the group not exposed to trauma recorded symptoms concordant with probable post-traumatic stress disorder (PTSD) (the estimated rate in the general population in Canada was 2.4 per cent).[8] Lawyers often work in situations of extreme stress (and therefore can experience the symptoms of extreme – and even traumatic – stress) whether there is trauma in their caseload or not.

A history of trauma

To understand the current research and language used in this field, it is useful to have an overview of its historical development. The modern history of our understanding of trauma is a story of constant development and waves of expansion, from the 'shell shock' of the First World War to survivor-led movements rejecting traditional psychiatric diagnoses.

As lawyers, our understanding of trauma is likely to be informed by the medical model because of the way in which medical diagnoses are relied upon in the justice system. In turn, we rely on experts to convince the court of our clients' injury or vulnerability. We work towards certainty, persuading the court of the unequivocal nature of their post-traumatic stress disorder (PTSD) diagnosis and, often, the cause of that traumatic stress.

However, an exploration of the recent history of psychological trauma illuminates its slipperiness as a concept. It has shape-shifted across the decades. What is considered trauma or a pathology by one group, at one time, in one society, is not fixed. We may need

---

8   Marie-Eve Leclerc, Jo-Anne Wemmers and Alain Brunet (2020), 'The unseen cost of justice: post-traumatic stress symptoms in Canadian lawyers', *Psychology, Crime & Law*, 26:1, 1-21, DOI: 10.1080/1068316X.2019.1611830/.

to follow the black letter of the contemporary definition of a psychiatric diagnosis in our litigation, but that is not necessarily the case in our own reflection on how trauma may be understood and experienced by ourselves and our colleagues.

Shell shock, veterans and war psychology

In 1915, during the First World War, psychologist Charles Myers wrote a paper for *The Lancet* medical journal which popularised the term 'shell shock' to describe the physical and psychological effects of the conflict. At the time, the government and military message was that those affected by shell shock would have developed some similar problems had they not gone to war, thus absolving them from the responsibility for these soldiers. Psychiatry's dominant view at the time was that mental illness was hereditary.

This is not to say that 'shell shock' is a wholly outdated concept. More recently, advances in neuroscience have shown physical injury to the brain following exposure to high-impact explosives causing chronic inflammation after low level blast effects.[9]

Changing psychiatric diagnosis

In 1980, PTSD was added to the 3rd edition of the *Diagnostic and statistical manual of mental disorders* (DSM) from the America Psychiatric Association (APA), from which psychiatrists across the world, including the UK, make their diagnoses. To qualify, the traumatic experience had to be 'outside the range of usual human experience' which would be 'markedly distressing to almost anyone'.

The requirement to compare in this way echoes the comparison in law with the hypothetical 'man on the Clapham omnibus', giving licence to the individual adjudicator (judge or psychiatrist) to decide what is a reasonable reaction.

The similarity between the professions does not end there. The evolution of psychiatric diagnosis is comparable to the evolution of common law. Committees made up of the most senior members of a

---

9 Sullivan et al, 'Cerebral perfusion is associated with blast exposure in military personnel without moderate or severe TBI', J Cereb Blood Flow Metab, 4 June 2020: www.darpa.mil/program/preventing-violent-explosive-neurologic-trauma; https://pubmed.ncbi.nlm.nih.gov/32580671/.

profession which was historically (and to an extent continues to be) limited to the most privileged of society.[10]

In 2013, the 5th edition the DSM (DSM-5) updated the criteria for diagnosis of PTSD to include 'indirect exposure to aversive details of the trauma, usually in the course of professional duties'. The other manners of exposure for a diagnosis are direct exposure; witnessing the trauma; or learning that a relative or close friend was exposed to the trauma.

The 5th edition also removed the necessity for the response to involve 'intense fear, helplessness or horror,' as this was not useful in predicting occurrence of PTSD.

The current DSM-5 criteria for PTSD are (summarised) as follows:[11]

- Exposure to a traumatic event directly; as a witness; learning that a relative or close friend experienced the trauma; or 'indirect exposure to aversive details of the trauma usually in the course of professional duties'.
- The traumatic event itself must fall within at least one of the following categories:
  - death;
  - threatened death;
  - actual or threatened serious injury;
  - actual or threatened sexual violence.
- With the symptoms from each of the following categories, lasting for at least a month, causing distress and/or preventing usual social or occupational activities:
  - re-experiencing;
  - avoidance;
  - negative thoughts or feelings;
  - arousal / reactivity.

(See 'secondary traumatic stress', p60.)

The use of these criteria also points to another important matter: it is possible (and even common) to fulfil the first criteria (exposure to trauma), *and* feel – *at the time* – intense fear, helplessness or horror, without going on to experience the 'post-trauma' symptoms. That might mean not experiencing any long-term effects, or only experiencing some.

---

10 Nathan Filer, *This Book Will Change Your Mind About Mental Health*, Faber & Faber, 2019.

11 *Diagnostic and statistical manual of mental disorders*, 5th edn, American Psychiatric Association, 2013.

This is not to say that psychiatric diagnoses are not important or helpful. They may provide an element of certainty which is useful in designing treatment and services and gaining access to such specialist treatment. It also provides certainty for the legal system to help protect rights or make a claim for injury. A diagnosis can also provide a sense of meaning, reassurance, or even identity for an individual. A diagnosis describes a particular set of experiences and so it allows people to connect with others who are having similar experiences and can be a useful shorthand to explain a person's experience.

However, diagnostic criteria are not an immutable definition of psychiatric distress. Although it is possible to receive a diagnosis of PTSD through secondary exposure to trauma in the workplace, one certainly does not need to fulfil all of the criteria to experiencing real and impactful distress from trauma. There are a whole range of 'subclinical' post-traumatic responses that may be more subtle but still very intrusive and disturbing without meeting the full PTSD criteria.

There is also, as with most psychological research, a bias towards existing privileged populations and particular groups. The research into traumatic stress is heavily focussed on war trauma. The United States Department of Veteran Affairs (VA) in the US spends billions of dollars on research each year on issues affecting veterans and is home to the National Centre for PTSD. Books are published written by ex-military personnel describing their experiences. We are, however, much less likely to read the accounts of those in the countries that the US – or indeed the UK – has invaded or colonised.

The medicalisation of distress risks overlooking the socio-political, systemic and interpersonal context. PTSD diagnoses are borne out of the capitalist, patriarchal, white supremacist system of knowledge, productivity and value. A limited set of diagnostic criteria cannot capture the range of experience of trauma as a result of, for example, racism, chronic poverty or workplace harrassment.

Beyond PTSD

Hysteria, forgetting and guilt

The history of trauma is also a history of oppression, forgetting and guilt. The prevalence and extent of sexual and domestic violence,[12] the trauma of racism and systemic trauma of all kinds has

---

12 For a detailed history read Judith Herman, *Trauma and recovery: the aftermath of violence—from domestic abuse to political terror*, 1992.

been repeatedly forgotten (by intentional cover-ups or wilful ignorance).[13]

The dominant systems leave out the experiences of the oppressed and the marginalised. For example, the 'post' in PTSD describes a situation where the trauma is over. Author and trauma specialist Resmaa Menakem, in his work on racism and trauma in America, uses the term 'pervasive traumatic stress disorder'[14] which arguably better accounts for the experience of those living in systems that oppress and violate them.

Similarly, many mental health 'patients' in the UK describe themselves as survivors of a system that medicalises and pathologises responses to trauma (most notably in the contested diagnoses of personality disorders).

In the 21st century, Bessel Van Der Kolk[15], Staci K Haines[16] and Resmaa Menakem[17] (among others) have reclaimed the body as the site for understanding and processing trauma. Alongside this, there has been change led by survivors and the critical psychiatry movement to bring trauma-informed practices into the mainstream and to include recognition of the wider context of mental health (such as social, political and economic factors).

For example, in 2018, the World Health Organisation's 'International Classification of Diseases' (ICD-11) – the other major diagnostic manual alongside the DSM – introduced a diagnosis of 'complex PTSD' (CPTSD or c-PTSD).[18] This diagnosis acknowledges the particular and severe effect of extremely threatening or horrid trauma from which escape is difficult or impossible, where all diagnostic criteria for PTSD are met, along with severe and persistent:

---

13 Herman describes Freud and his contemporaries when they seemed to uncover a huge amount of child abuse in analysis: they re-wrote the story, that it was the defect of hysterical women.

14 *My Grandmother's Hands: Racialised Trauma and the Pathway to Mending Our Hearts and Bodies*, Central Recovery Press, 201, p15.

15 *The body keeps the score: brain, mind, and body in the healing of trauma*, Penguin Random House, 2015.

16 *The politics of trauma: somatics, healing, and social justice*, North Atlantic Books, 2019.

17 *My Grandmother's hands: racialized trauma and the pathway to mending our hearts and bodies*, Central Recovery Press, 2017.

18 Some feel this diagnosis is more appropriate and compassionate 'label' than BPD, considering not 'what is wrong with you?' but 'what happened to you?'. World Health Organization. (2018). *International classification of diseases for mortality and morbidity statistics* (11th Revision). Retrieved from https://icd.who.int/browse11/l-m/en

- problems in regulation of mood;
- belief about oneself as diminished, defeated or worthless;
- feelings of shame, guilt or failure related to the traumatic event;
- difficulties sustaining relationships and feeling close to others.

Towards a broader understanding of trauma and its prevalence

Recent research[19] estimates that around a third of adults have experienced one traumatic event[20] and a nationwide NHS survey in 2014 found one in twenty participants screened positive for PTSD (with only half of those receiving mental health treatment).

A 2019 study in *The Lancet* of a population-representative cohort of young adults born in 1994–1995 in England and Wales found a rate of 31.1 per cent of participants reporting trauma exposure and 7.8 per cent having experienced PTSD by age 18.

The diagnostic criteria for trauma-related 'disorders' use narrow definitions of 'trauma'. However in psychology and popular understanding there is a broader meaning.

Guidance from mental health charity Mind[21] describes trauma as personal, and focusses on the effect of the experience. A traumatic *experience* is one where you feel, for example, any of:

- frightened;
- under threat;
- humiliated;
- rejected;
- abandoned;
- invalidated;
- unsafe;
- unsupported;
- trapped;
- ashamed;
- powerless.

---

19 'The epidemiology of trauma and post-traumatic stress disorder in a representative cohort of young people in England and Wales', *The Lancet*, Volume 6, Issue 3, P247–256, 1 March 2019: https://doi.org/10.1016/S2215-0366(19)30031-8; Nicola T Fear, Sally Bridge, Stephani Hatch, Victoria Hawkins, Simon Wessely, 'Posttraumatic stress disorder', *Adult psychiatric morbidity survey 2014*, chapter 4: https://files.digital.nhs.uk/pdf/0/8/adult_psychiatric_study_ch4_web.pdf.

20 As per the DCM definition of a traumatic event.

21 *Trauma*, Mind, 2020: www.mind.org.uk/media-a/4149/trauma-2020.pdf.

This expanded definition is more inclusive and better allows for the trauma of, for example, discrimination and domestic violence by way of coercive control.

'Opening the floodgates'

Lawyers working in personal injury law (or those who still remember their academic legal studies on this topic) will know of the arbitrary limits on recovery for psychiatric injury (or 'nervous shock' as it is historically known) – limits designed to keep the metaphorical 'floodgates' closed to potential claimants. From the first 'nervous shock' case[22] which declined to extend liability for negligence because of the risk of false claims for 'mere sudden terror', case-law on psychiatric harm has developed into a 'patchwork quilt of distinctions which are difficult to justify'.[23] The court sets a high bar for a 'shocking' event, requiring an exceptional incident (for which even brain haemorrhage or neonatal death do not necessarily qualify) and it is notoriously difficult to succeed in a claim for psychiatric injury as a secondary victim (ie as a witness rather than the direct victim).

One wonders if the judicial scepticism has affected our attitude to trauma as it affects those that work within the legal system. Perhaps there is a fear of 'opening the floodgates' to the torrent of vicarious trauma. Instead, we rely on a systemic 'forgetting' of those who choose to leave the profession, and ignoring the distress and poor quality of life of some of those who stay. To recognise the potential severity of the situation would expose the pervasiveness of trauma in the legal profession.

Bringing greater awareness of these issues to the legal profession will necessitate an honest examination of the potential severity of the situation. It is likely that such a reckoning will require action.

Primary trauma in the workplace

As set out above, the diagnostic criteria for PTSD under DSM-5 now include 'repeated or extreme exposure to aversive details of the traumatic event(s)'.

---

22   *Victorian Railway Commissioners v James and Mary Coultas* (1888) 13 App Cas 222.

23   *White v CC SYP* [1999] 2 AC 455: Lord Steyn, 'the law on the recovery of compensation for pure psychiatric harm is a patchwork quilt of distinctions which are difficult to justify'.

It is likely, therefore, that the body of research on PTSD and secondary / vicarious traumatic stress will converge to some extent. In practice, however, the distinction drawn between the two tends to be a difference between occupational transmission of trauma (secondary) as compared to incidental or collateral 'victims' of trauma (eg witness to a car crash or aftermath of a natural disaster in a non-professional capacity).

Lawyers working on a caseload including accounts of abuse, assault and torture are likely to review details of traumatic events on a daily basis. Some professionals working in the frontline of the justice system are often exposed to primary as well as secondary trauma. It is, sadly, also possible that a lawyer will have a primary experience of trauma in the course of their duties. For example, in a violent police station setting, receiving threats from an aggrieved client or witnessing a client experiencing a mental health crisis. The relative unlikelihood of this occurring in legal settings and the overwhelming unpreparedness of lawyers when such incidents *do* occur, is a matter of concern – and it is likely to have a significant bearing on an individual's ability to process and recover from that primary trauma. In this context, it is a matter of horror and deep regret that whilst we have been writing this book there has been a knife attack at a London law firm. The attack, in which a knifeman threatened to kill an immigration solicitor, is believed to be directly motivated by comments made by the current home secretary, Priti Patel.[24]

---

24 https://www.theguardian.com/politics/2020/oct/10/lawyers-claim-knife-attack-at-law-firm-was-inspired-by-priti-patels-rhetoric

CHAPTER 3

Vicarious trauma

Trauma is contagious[1]

We are lawyers and professionals. We are also human beings living in the world. Each of us brings our own history and experience that cannot be separated from how we do the work that we do. We use our intellectual expertise in our day-to-day work, but our 'thinking minds' are not separate from our psychological processing of emotions and our overall physical wellbeing.

Conversations on wellbeing at work, and particularly in the legal profession, usually focus on stress as a product of the pressure of working as a lawyer, with little or no consideration of the *content* of the work itself. For many lawyers, the content of the documents, statements and accounts of their clients will have little effect on their wellbeing beyond the stress of the work generally. However, for social justice and legal aid lawyers – as well as others working in areas, such as personal injury – it is not simply a case of filing deadlines, billing targets and irate judges that affects stress and wellbeing.

'Every Saturday morning I used to cry. I'd have harrowing meetings all week where you are not meant to react even if you are upset or sick. So on Saturday mornings I'd purposefully read things that I knew would make me cry. I needed to get it all out, and that usually did help.'

Solicitor

Why do we feel trauma that isn't happening to us?

Our ability to be moved by events that are not directly happening to us is an important part of being human. It enriches our relationships and our lives through how we engage with art or stories. It provides a sense of community and connection, with family, close friends and other important connections.

It makes sense that as 'social animals' we feel the pain of others in our group, as a way to create a sense of collective care for the survival of the group. It is also important in our work as lawyers to have a sense of empathy with our clients. Empathetic connection is often critical to the development of a relationship of trust with our

---

1 Judith Herman, *Trauma and recovery: the aftermath of violence – from domestic abuse to political terror*, 1992, p140.

clients, many of whom have experienced chronic or acute failings by the people or institutions in which they have placed their trust.

In this context, it becomes necessary to build and develop an emotional currency with clients, one that allows us to take instructions and build rapport. But as with all currencies, this involves a system of acceptance and exchange on both sides, leaving us vulnerable to the emotions and traumas of our clients that are shared through that exchange. This is sometimes described as, 'the cost of caring'.[2]

> ... compassion fatigue is specific to individuals working in fields where *interpersonal engagement with clients in need is a major component of service delivery* (e.g. attorneys, mental health professionals, medical doctors).[3]

There is no one reason why working with trauma affects us (or does not) – but there are a number of mechanisms that are likely at play in the process of vicarious traumatisation. (See further, chapter 6.)

What makes us empathetic?

Mirror neurons

'Mirror neurons' were discovered by accident in the 1990s in Italy, when scientists were measuring brain activity in primates and noticed that there was activity in the brain area of the monkey associated with a particular task (picking up a raisin) when the animal observed the researcher doing that task.[4]

Neurons are nerves that create the chains that send communication through the brain and the rest of the nervous system via electrical impulses and chemicals.

Motor neurons are responsible for sending and receiving messages regarding movement. Motor mirror neurons are activated when a person (or animal) observes another carrying out an action, mirroring the brain activity implicated in that action without actually carrying out that action themselves. Research is still in a relatively

---

2 CR Figley (1995), *Compassion fatigue: Toward a new understanding of the costs of caring.*.

3 Megan Zwisohn, Wayne Handley, Danielle Winters, Alyssa Reiter, 'Vicarious trauma in public service lawyering: how chronic exposure to trauma affects the brain and body', *Richmond Public Interest Law Review*, Volume 22, Issue 2, Article 9 p283 (emphasis added).

4 G di Pellegrino, L Fadiga, L Fogassi, V Gallese, G Rizzolatti, 'Understanding motor events: a neurophysiological study', *Exp Brain Res.* 1992; 91(1):176–180.

early stage, but neuroscientists are investigating[5] the potential role of mirror neurons in a variety of areas including learning, self-awareness and empathy.[6]

What science is starting to discover and prove, is that emotions, no matter how much they feel that way, are not wholly personal, and neither is trauma.

Personal experience

We may have experienced the same kind of traumatic incident that our client is recounting or that we are reading about or watching, and hearing the details of that incident may take is right back to our own visceral memory of our own trauma.

Additionally, empathy is something that we can practice intentionally, and may develop more capacity for as we develop our skills to be more effective lawyers.

Imagination

We might also have strong empathy because of our ability to imagine an experience.

From research using fMRI scanning we know that neural 'pain processing' areas are activated when a person is asked to imagine themselves in a painful situation and when a person is asked to imagine another in a painful situation.[7] Perhaps unsurprisingly, participants rated higher levels of pain and distress in the research when they were asked to imagine themselves in pain.

It is possible that this is in fact an exacerbating feature of vicarious trauma in the legal profession because of the nature of the role, in contrast to others working with a similar client group.

When we write a witness statement we embody the 'I' who has experienced (or perhaps perpetrated) the trauma, asking the client (and ourselves) 'how does this action follow that', and 'where are we

5 Valeria Gazzola, Lisa Aziz-Zadeh and Christian Keysers, 'Empathy and the soma-totopic auditory mirror system in humans', *Current Biology*, Volume 16, Issue 18, P1824–1829, 19 September 2006: https://doi.org/10.1016/j.cub.2006.07.072.

6 Christian Keysers, *The empathic brain: how the discovery of mirror neurons changes our understanding of human nature*, Createspace Independent Publishing Platform, 2011.

7 PL Jackson, E Brunet, AN Meltzoff and J Decety, 'Empathy examined through the neural mechanisms involved in imagining how I feel versus how you feel pain: An event-related fMRI study', *Neuropsychologia*, (2006) 44, 752–761: https://doi:10.1016/j.neuropsychologia.2005.07.015.

on the map', making site visits and examining photographs and video footage in detail.

> 'A colleague once explained it really well to me. When you are doing that work you are visualising it, using your imagination as if you are reading a novel. It isn't just a case of processing and it going away. It creates a picture in your mind.'
>
> *Solicitor*

Alternatively, in cases where we represent the individual who is perpetrating or alleged to have perpetrated the trauma (commonly in criminal defence, but also in other cases), it is also traumatic to imagine the point of view of the person committing a violent act. Even though we do not ever believe that we might do something so violent, our imaginations can take us there, both on purpose in drafting a statement or thinking through weaknesses in an account, and – more problematically – unintentionally, with intrusive thoughts or nightmares.

> **CW: self-harm**
>
> 'As a trainee I had to go through medical records of a client who had committed a crime and had been sectioned. I had to look through three or four years of daily contact logs where the client was being reviewed every 15 mins. The notes were very detailed, about his state of mind, the comments he was making about the serious crimes he committed, and details of self-harming.
>
> I don't think at the time I realised how awful it was and it still has an impact on me years later. Had I been later on in my career I probably would have just said I don't want to see all of these details because it was pretty horrific. Now I'm reflecting on it I realise it affected me, but I don't think I did at the time. Over the last few years it has come back to me. Now I wonder if that was a suitable task for a junior lawyer. I was working for a very good and responsible supervisor at the time, which makes me wonder how much worse it is for people who do not have proper supervision.'
>
> *Solicitor*

Burnout and 'compassion fatigue' are more prevalent where our work conflicts with our values, for example working with perpetrators of crime. In a sector where generally we believe absolutely in the principle of a good defence or legal representation for all, equal before the law, that does not mean that the actions of the people we represent don't also have the potential to cause us damage.

Summary

Trauma, including vicarious trauma, is often experienced as if it were an individual, personal problem. This experience is reinforced and validated by the legal system. However, the very existence of empathy reminds us that this is not the case. Humans are relational beings. Trauma is a relational phenomenon. The response must also be relational.

'Self-care' is therefore perhaps not always a helpful term. It requires collective action. It is within the context of collective / systemic / organisational support that individual self-care takes place. This work neither begins nor ends with the individual, although some responsibility – and control – lies with the individual.

There is a balance to be struck between promoting the collective and structural impact of the work and the power each individual has to address that impact.

Compassion fatigue, vicarious trauma and secondary traumatic stress

Compassion fatigue

Early researchers (in the 1980s and 1990s) described 'compassion fatigue'[8] as an effect of working in the helping professions, as distinct from 'burnout', which is caused by environmental and organisational factors and applies to all professions not just those exposed to trauma or distress.

---

8 CR Figley (1995), *Compassion fatigue: Toward a new understanding of the costs of caring.*

Vicarious trauma

'Vicarious trauma' as a term was coined by McCann and Pearlman[9] to describe the cognitive changes in professionals exposed to their clients' belief system about themselves and the world, resulting in a disruption to the internal schema (for example, from seeing the world as inherently benign to believing it to be inherently malevolent).

Secondary traumatic stress

'Secondary traumatic stress' (STS) describes the experience of symptoms that mirror post-traumatic stress disorder (PTSD) caused by indirect exposure to trauma (as opposed to direct exposure).

Precise distinctions between vicarious trauma and STS have not been resolved in research literature. An exploration of the conceptual differences are beyond remit of this book. We have set out working definitions based on commonly used meanings to provide a linguistic framework and shared language. However, there is some difficulty in comparing research and resources because of the lack of universal definition. Added to that, the research into the legal profession is still limited (albeit a slowly growing body of literature). It is therefore helpful to have an understanding of the study of vicarious trauma across other professions where the research base is more established.

STS symptoms, which mirror those of primary trauma, are generally categorised into three subgroups: intrusion (including elevated heart rate when thinking about work, seeming to relive the trauma experienced by clients, disturbing dreams); avoidance (emotional numbness, gaps in memory, loss of interest in others), substance misuse and arousal (feeling 'jumpy', being easily annoyed, having trouble sleeping and expecting something bad to happen).

While the distinctions between vicarious trauma and STS have not been resolved in the literature, Molnar et al set out a useful

---

9 L McCann and L Pearlman (1990) 'Vicarious traumatization: a framework for understanding tile psychological effects of working with victims', *Journal of Traumatic Stress*, 3(1), 131–149. https://doi.org/10.1007/BF00975140/..

conceptual framework encompassing both.[10] Those researchers conceptualised vicarious trauma as both a mode of exposure (ie indirect exposure to a traumatic incident); a process (that results in a change in world view); and a spectrum of affective and behavioural responses, which include both negative outcomes (eg STS, compassion fatigue) and positive outcomes (eg post-traumatic growth).[11]

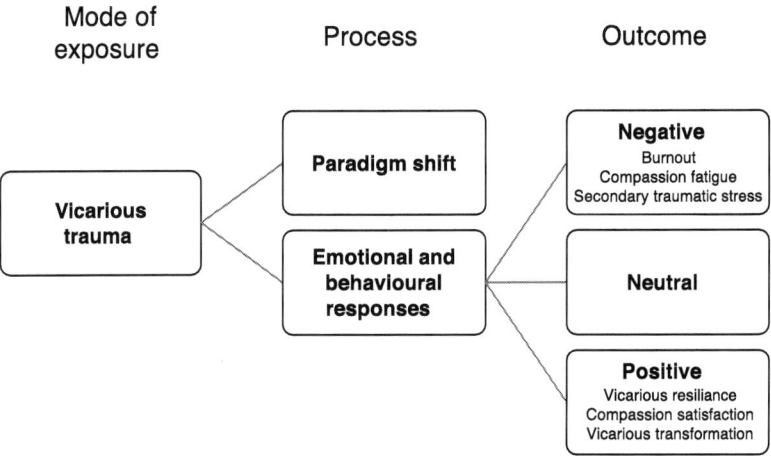

Adapted from the framework of Molnar et al.[12]

A mode of exposure

In this sense, 'vicarious trauma' is a neutral term to describe the mode of exposure by which lawyers (or any individual) is exposed to sensory / cognitive input of a traumatic nature.

10 BE Molnar, G Sprang, KD Killian, R Gottfried, V Emery: http://orcid.org/ Molnar Bride Beth E.; ORCID: http://orcid.org/0000-0002-5628-2989, B. E. A. I.-O. (2017). Advancing science and practice for vicarious traumatization/ secondary traumatic stress: A research agenda. *Special Issue: Secondary Traumatic Stress, Compassion Fatigue, and Vicarious Trauma*, 23(2), 129–142. https://doi.org/http://dx.doi.org/10.1037/trm0000122

11 L Harms (2015), *Understanding Trauma and Resilience*, Palgrave; K Cohen and P Collens (2012) 'The impact of trauma work – a meta-synthesis on vicarious trauma and vicarious trauma growth' Psychological Trauma: Theory, Research, Practice, and Policy, 5(6), 570–580. https://doi.org/10.1037/a0030388/. L Harms (2015), Understanding Trauma and Resilience, Palgrave; K Cohen and P Collens (2012) 'The impact of trauma work – a meta-synthesis on vicarious trauma and vicarious trauma growth' *Psychological Trauma: Theory, Research, Practice, and Policy*, 5(6), 570–580. https://doi.org/10.1037/a0030388/.

12 Molnar et al, *Traumatology*, (2017) Vol 23, No 2, 129–142.

It should, therefore, be in commonplace usage in the sectors of the legal profession that deal with traumatic content. In those workplaces with a human resources (HR) officer or team, it should be part of their everyday vocabulary. It should form part of every induction, every pathway of legal education – from accredited police station representatives to the judiciary.

Currently, vicarious trauma is not usually used as a neutral term, but perhaps it should be. Being able to describe the fact of our exposure to trauma should not be controversial. It is not a matter of who is and isn't affected, rather it is a fact of life for all lawyers working in the traditionally publicly funded areas of law, as well as many others.

The processes of vicarious trauma

Change in world view

When a person experiences a severe traumatic shock, it can feel as if their life has split into two: the 'before' and 'after'. Before the incident, this person may have felt more or less safe in their world, hopeful and able to make plan. Afterwards, they may feel a total absence of security, like the ground has been pulled out from underneath them. Plans made in the 'before' time seem absurd, irrelevant or impossible in the 'after' time.

With the more gradual effect of vicarious trauma, such a change may not be so dramatic. There is often no distinct 'before' or 'after'. Instead, over time, we realise that our outlook on the world, our feelings of safety, or even our personality, seem to have changed.

In our professional lives, these feelings of hopelessness or a change in view of the world can lead to, for example:

- a feeling of disconnection from our values and our motivation to do the work;
- cynicism, lack of sympathy or lack of engagement with our clients;
- cynicism towards management and/or systems;
- feeling like a failure or imposter;
- guilt.

In our personal lives, this negative paradigm shift affects our quality of life, habits and social engagement.

For many lawyers, the work does not stop with the cases on their current list. Engaging with the work often means being involved in activism more broadly. The lack of hope that this paradigm shift can create can serve to reduce feelings of connection and agency, possibly leading to lower engagement with activism. Conversely, engaging in activism may keep a person connected to the values that drive them and be a protective factor against the negative effects of vicarious trauma.

A range of responses

Finally, there are a range of outcomes or effects that might be described as negative (those which we may be most concerned about, and which will form the majority of the next section of this book) and positive (rarely considered but equally important).

The negative responses that we will consider here are:

- burnout;
- compassion fatigue;
- STS/PTSD.

We will also consider the positive:

- vicarious resilience;
- post-traumatic growth.

For lawyers, there might be positive responses beyond these, related to being a part of collective change, bearing witness, achieving accountability, political change or resistance.

This range of responses may ring true for many lawyers, and certainly may be true for some lawyers some of the time. Without wishing to be too cynical or pessimistic, it is worth noting that some people who feel unaffected at work may experience the effect of the work outside of the office, or even at a later date (after leaving practice, or while taking a break). The effect may also be less obviously or clearly connected to work. Physical symptoms in particular are less likely to be attributed to vicarious trauma in a world where 'physical' and 'mental' health are understood as distinct areas – a false distinction when it comes to the effects of trauma especially.

Even if you are a lawyer who has never experienced the negative effect of vicarious trauma, it is important to know the risks to better resource yourself for the future, minimise risk and, crucially, to support your colleagues to create a better, more understanding and reflective environment. This is an even greater imperative for lawyers in supervisory roles.

Practice: noticing the body

You might have started to reflect on your own experience as you have been reading this book. If it feels okay to do so right now, try taking a moment to pay attention to your body and what you are experiencing. You could try a brief 'body scan'.

Start either at the top of the head or in the feet and scan through one body part at a time. Not doing anything, just noticing what's there: tension, tingling, numbness, blankness, heat, coolness, discomfort, pain, ease, lightness, comfort. Whatever you find, can you pay attention for a moment or two, before moving on to the next part?

If there is any body part that does not feel safe to pay attention to, for whatever reason, then you are invited to simply skip over that part.

By making a habit of checking in with our body, we are better able to notice how we are reacting to what we are experiencing (including the experience of reading this book).

CHAPTER 4

Vicarious trauma and the legal profession

There is arguably no more fitting epithet to the 'traditional' identity of a lawyer than Descartes' infamous 'cogito ergo sum': 'I think, therefore I am' (especially given the profession's penchant for Latin). This ethos permeates legal education and practice today. In law, our ability to override our emotions in order to assess cases dispassionately is usually considered an asset.

> Reason is the life of the law, nay the common law itself is nothing else but reason. Law . . . is the perfection of reason.
>
> Edward Coke

What changes if instead we bring our full *emotional selves* to the law? What changes when we acknowledge the role of *emotion* in our legal practice (rather than ignore, deny or minimise it)?

It is difficult to bring trauma awareness into the legal profession for many reasons, not least because it involves bringing our attention to our bodies. This can be difficult because of the trauma itself, which can make the body feel an unsafe place to 'be'; because of messages we receive about the importance or value of our bodies from society or family; or because we are simply so unused to paying attention to the body.

What is the difference for lawyers?

Lawyers are 'trained to assume that the only things relevant to their relationships with their clients are how well they know the law and how well they can read and apply it'.[1]

On the one hand, we are to remain dispassionate, to advise on the merits of the case alone. To make difficult decisions and advise on the evidence as it can be proven (rather than what 'feels' right). This is the kind of training we are given.

However, in reality, lawyers working in the fields of legal aid, social justice or survivors of injury quickly learn that a certain amount of emotion or empathy, described above as a form of 'emotional currency', is almost always exchanged. Sometimes this has to happen very quickly – a lawyer trying to gain the trust of a child or distressed person at a police station, for example – or it may happen over many months or even years of working on a case.

---

1   MA Silver, S Portnoy and JK Peters (2004), 'Stress, burnout, vicarious trauma, and other emotional realities in the lawyer/client relationship: A panel discussion', *Touro Law Review*, 19, 847–873.

'I think the main thing with the vicarious trauma and those kind of issues is that there just is no preparation for it; all of a sudden you might be in a meeting with a client to take their witness statement and they are telling you something horrific. You're not their counsellor, but equally you cannot just be sobbing. It is a weird experience. Most people who work in this kind of area are sympathetic and find these issues upsetting, but you can't really be outwardly upset by them. You cannot be upset in front of clients, in the office you cannot just sit there crying. It is very odd, very difficult.'

Paralegal

Historically, this is a topic absent from the education, training and development for 'trauma-exposed' lawyers. The tide is turning, but the lack of this sort of education can lead to – at best – a blind spot as to the risks of vicarious trauma or, in some organisations, an active denial of this as an issue with negative consequences for speaking out about these kinds of experiences.

For example, if a junior solicitor's time-recording has reduced dramatically, do you enforce punitive measures or do you provide support, examine their caseload, find out what other factors might be involved?

In this book we will examine some of the factors that are affecting the legal profession, including:

- lack of training – legal education and training to operate in an emotional vacuum;
- lack of acknowledgment of the phenomena for lawyers;
- lack of supervision (see p147);
- lack of reflection in practice (see p115);
- lawyers as problem-solvers (see p76, mindfulness);
- mental health stigma in the legal profession;
- the professional relationship – the need to gain a client's trust often in pressured situations or in the aftermath of serious trauma increases the need for an emotional exchange.

Whose responsibility is it?

As we make clear in this book, the impact of vicarious trauma is not solely an individual one. The responsibility for addressing both the risk and the actual effects of vicarious trauma is also not an individual one. Ultimately, actively traumatised lawyers will be far less able to act effectively for their clients; lawyers experiencing burnout will be far less able to act effectively for their clients; and, what's more, lawyers doing vital work in the interests of individual and social justice deserve to expect a reasonable quality of life within the workplace and outside of it.

We make the case that there are both effective and powerful ways to address the risk and effects on an individual case while at the same time being very clear that the individual must not take on this responsibility alone.

Solicitors firms, law centres and other employers have a clear duty of care towards their employees for risks faced in the workplace. Self-employed barristers – who practice in chambers, as part of a collective group of barristers – owe duties of care to their pupils. It is in the best interests of all lawyers, regardless of duty of care, to work in non-traumatised environments, whether that is in a small niche chambers or a nationwide large personal injury firm. It is also in the best interests of our clients that we collectively address the impact of vicarious trauma and burnout.

How prevalent is vicarious trauma in the wider legal system?

Despite the frequent contact lawyers have with traumatic material and traumatised clients, vicarious trauma and secondary traumatic stress is little studied in the legal profession.

At the end of a difficult case, the members of a jury may be given a lifetime exemption from serving on a jury again. It is considered that they have fulfilled their civic duty. A judge may decide that counselling support is needed at the end of a case.

However, the judge, clerk, court staff, security staff and lawyers involved in the case will be back in court the next day. The lawyers and judges may be going back to their offices or chambers to review the papers – and traumatic details – for another case that same day.

There has been some research into the effects of working with traumatised clients or traumatic material in the justice system. Negative impacts have been found in jurors,[2] police officers[3] and prison staff.[4]

Unfortunately, despite the fact that Saakvitne and Pearlman[5] identified criminal lawyers as a profession particularly at risk of developing vicarious trauma in the early 1990s, there has been little research carried out in lawyers, and only a handful of small-scale studies on lawyers in the UK. Those studies that have been conducted are self-reporting and of a cross-sectional, correlational design.

What can the current research tell us?

International research on lawyers' experience of trauma provides the following insights:

- Lawyers working with traumatised clients seem to have poorer mental health than other professionals working with similar client groups (eg mental health professionals and social workers).[6] They also have higher rates of secondary trauma and burnout.
- In one 2003 study, the lawyers interviewed expressed relief that the fact that this issue was being researched was an indication that they were 'not the only one'.[7] The lawyers tended to attribute the negative symptoms to lack of preparedness in dealing with traumatised client groups; lack of forum to share and discuss experiences; and a frustration with the systems within which lawyers work (including hostile court and law enforcement staff, and indifferent senior colleagues).

2 M Lonergan, ME Leclerc, M Descamps, S Pigeon, A Brunet (2016) 'Prevalence and severity of trauma- and stressor-related symptoms among jurors: a review' *Journal of Criminal Justice*, 47, 51–61. https://doi.org/10.1016/j.jcrimjus.2016.07.003/.

3 D Turgoose and L Maddox (2017), 'Predictors of compassion fatigue in mental health professionals: a narrative review', *Traumatology*, 23(2), 172–185. https://doi.org/10.1037/trm0000116/.

4 B Thomas (2012) *Predictors of Vicarious Trauma and Secondary Traumatic Stress Among Correctional Officers.*

5 KW Saakvitne, and LA Pearlman, Transforming the pain: a workbook on vicarious traumatization, WW Norton & Company Inc, 1996.

6 A Levin and S Greisberg (2003), 'Vicarious Trauma in Attorneys', *Pace Law Review*, 24(1), 245–847. .

7 Levin and Greisberg, 2003.

- In an Australian study from 2016, not only were lawyers experiencing more vicarious trauma, they also measured significantly higher levels of depression, anxiety and stress. The researchers also considered whether personality differences might account for the difference in mental health but found no statistically significant difference in personality traits.[8]
- Lawyers working with trauma also, unsurprisingly, measured unfavourably compared to 'non-trauma' lawyers. Vrklevski and Franklin[9] in Australia compared criminal lawyers (who are exposed to trauma) and lawyers working with little to no exposure to trauma. Significant differences were found between the two groups in their scores on the Vicarious Trauma Scale (VTS) as well as Depression and Stress Scale. Across the groups, trauma history was associated with higher vicarious trauma measures.
- A study of 476 Canadian lawyers compared three groups of lawyers: one working with no trauma in their caseload; a second with some; and a third with a main caseload of trauma.[10] They found:
  - worse physical health for those lawyers with trauma exposure;
  - an increase in PTSD symptom severity as trauma exposure increased;
  - 15 per cent of the highly exposed lawyers met the diagnostic criteria for probable post-traumatic stress disorder (PTSD).
- A small pilot study of asylum lawyers in UK found that 34.3 per cent met PTSD criteria; 51.4% had scores suggesting "partial PTSD"; and that fewer years' experience correlated to higher scores.[11] These recent findings are particularly stark. As the researchers note, this is a small sample but supports the argument for much wider research to be undertaken.

8 G Maguire and MK Byrne (2017), 'The law is not as blind as it seems: relative rates of vicarious trauma among lawyers and mental health professionals', *Psychiatry, Psychology and Law*, 24(2), 233–243. https://doi.org/10.1080/132187 19.2016.1220037/.

9 PL Vrklevski and J Franklin (2008), 'Vicarious trauma: The impact on solicitors of exposure to traumatic material', *Traumatology*, 14(1), 106–118. https://doi.org/10.1177/1534765607309961/

10 Marie-Eve Leclerc, Jo-Anne Wemmers and Alain Brunet (2020), 'The unseen cost of justice: post-traumatic stress symptoms in Canadian lawyers', *Psychology, Crime & Law*, 26:1, 1-21, DOI: 10.1080/1068316X.2019.1611830

11 Line Rønning, Jocelyn Blumberg & Jesper Dammeyer (2020): Vicarious traumatisation in lawyers working with traumatised asylum seekers: a pilot study, *Psychiatry, Psychology and Law*, DOI: 10.1080/13218719.2020.1742238/.

- In surveys by the Junior Lawyers Division (JLD) of The Law Society:
  - In their 2019[12] survey of members, almost a third of the 1,803 respondents to the survey worked with vulnerable clients.[13] Over half of those respondents reported experiencing mental ill-health over the prior month (53 per cent of those working with the 'vulnerable' client group, compared to 46 per cent of those not working with that group). Over one-fifth (22.9 per cent) of respondents working with vulnerable clients regularly felt unable to cope, compared to 17.3 per cent of those not working with this client group.
  - In the 2018[14] JLD survey, of the 959 respondents, a quarter were working with vulnerable clients. These lawyers were more likely to 'regularly' feel unable to cope and to experience mental health problems over the prior month. Just under 23 per cent of this group reported that their employers provided mental health help, guidance or support, compared to just under 43 per cent of those not working with vulnerable clients.
  - The first JLD survey, in 2017, found that 26 per cent of respondents had been 'severely' or 'extremely severely' stressed in the preceding month.

Summary

- It is clear that exposure to trauma through legal casework does lead to negative effects of vicarious trauma (when compared to lawyers not working with trauma).
- The research shows the outcomes are worse for lawyers compared with other professions dealing with similar clients and trauma.
- Not everyone exposed to secondary trauma develops traumatic stress symptoms.

12 *JLD resilience and wellbeing survey report 2019*, The Law Society, April 2019: www.lawsociety.org.uk/topics/junior-lawyers/jld-resilience-and-wellbeing-survey-report-2019.

13 Defined as vulnerable by virtue of age, mental or physical health difficulty, as a result of being in custody, through lack of capacity, through experience of trauma, or who are vulnerable for any other reason.

14 *Resilience and wellbeing report. Junior Lawyers Division*, The Law Society, April 2018: https://communities.lawsociety.org.uk/Uploads/p/d/i/jld-resilience-and-wellbeing-survey-report-2018.pdf.

- The likelihood of developing traumatic stress symptoms is not solely explained by levels of exposure to it (indeed, some findings suggest no significant link[15]).
- The current research does not examine any potential disproportionate impact on lawyers who belong to marginalised groups.
- Therefore, to understand this phenomenon fully, examination must be made of other factors, such as individual difference in resilience and personality traits, as well as external support and behavioural responses.

Notes of caution

- What is defined as 'trauma' in the studies is limited to certain areas of law (eg criminal law, asylum practitioners, etc) – but there are many other areas of law that will frequently deal with traumatic incidents as part of their case facts (eg personal injury and clinical negligence), as part of the client's life story (eg housing), or where caseloads may be very mixed (eg family) or in others where infrequent exposure to traumatic details is likely (eg wills).
- There is no real binary of lawyers in the legal aid and social welfare sector who work with trauma and those who do not. There are also lawyers who work outside of the traditionally legal aid funded sector who are exposed to significant trauma in their workload.
- All the research above has been conducted by voluntary completion of self-reported questionnaires. It is possible, therefore, that there is a discrepancy between the way the respondents view themselves on the day of the survey and the reality of day-to-day impact. Second, there is also a possibility that those experiencing worse effects of vicarious trauma self-select to respond to the survey, meaning that the rates and percentages are higher than in the general population of lawyers as a whole.
- Most of the available research tells us about the *general* experience at a population level and not the individual level.

15 R Ivicic and R Motta (2017), 'Variables associated with secondary traumatic stress among mental health professionals', *Traumatology*, 23(2), 196–204. http://psycnet.apa.org/doi/10.1037/trm0000065/.

CHAPTER 5

Physiological effects and impacts of vicarious trauma

continued

Secondary traumatic stress   60

Hyper-arousal   61

'Flight' response • 'Fight' response • Re-experiencing • Reactivity (fight or flight) • Cognitive effects of hyper-arousal

Hypo-arousal   62

'Freeze' response • 'Appease/fawn' response • 'Faint/flop/dissociative' response • Avoidance • Numbing • Cognitive effects of hypo-arousal

Physical effects of secondary traumatic stress   65

Post-traumatic stress disorder   66

Compassion is an unstable emotion. It needs to be translated into action, or it withers . . . People don't become inured to what they are shown – if that's the right way to describe what happens – because of the quantity of images dumped on them. It is passivity that dulls feeling. The states described as apathy, moral or emotional anaesthesia, are full of feelings; the feelings are rage and frustration.

Susan Sontag, *Regarding the pain of others*[1]

Practice: taking care

As we begin a more detailed exploration of the effects and impacts of vicarious trauma, we might feel a reaction to some of the content. This is absolutely okay. You are invited to return at any time to your 'anchor' (see p11). If you notice that you are feeling any overwhelming sensations, thoughts or feelings, you might want to pause your reading for a while.

Stress reactions – including traumatic stress reactions – are physiological responses to threats. We will discuss how traumatic stress can (and must) be understood in our current socio-political and structural contexts later in the book.

First, however, we will explore the biological, internal, responses. The following is intended as an overview and not a detailed account. More resources are included at appendix B.

Physiological stress response

When our body receives an experience understood as a threat (to our survival, or to some other important aspect of our lives) a stress response is triggered. For example, you are running late for work. When you arrive at the station platform, your train is already there and the beeps have just started sounding, signalling that the doors are closing. Your body jumps into action, your muscles fire and your heart rate increases. You might experience tunnel vision – the only thing you can see is the gap between the doors. You jump onto the train with just a second to spare. Your breath is heavy and maybe your hands are shaking a little.

1 Susan Sontag, *Regarding the pain of others*, Picador, 2003.

By the time the train arrives at the next station, your body understands that the threat (of missing the train, arriving late, being told off by your supervisor or a judge) has passed, your breathing and heart rate have returned to normal and you might even be feeling a little euphoric!

What is happening in your brain?

Thinking brain vs survival brain

Our 'thinking' brain can reason that we are safe, while at the same time our 'survival' brain is sending messages to our body to tell us that we are not.

If you make a fist with one hand by wrapping your fingers around your thumb, you have a 'handy' 3D diagram of the human brain.[2]

- Thinking brain:
  - The fingers = the cortex.
  - Lower parts of the fingers/knuckle and fingernails = the prefrontal cortex (the area behind forehead).
- Survival brain:
  - Thumb = limbic system.
  - Palm = brain stem.
  - Wrist = spinal cord.

To simplify, the fingers represent the 'thinking' area of the brain; and the rest of the hand and wrist represent the 'survival' areas of the brain.

Thinking brain

Cortex

The legal profession is dominated by the processing we do in the cortex – the thinking, intellectual brain. We seek out solutions to problems; we arrange arguments in the most logical and persuasive manner possible; we may rely on the effect of emotion in our case, but we do so largely in a controlled way. This part of the brain controls:

- language;
- imagination;

---

2   The 'triune brain' – MacLean, 1990; the 'hand model of the brain' – Dr Dan Siegal.

- analytic thought;
- planning for multiple future scenarios;
- taking in complex data and processing it.

Pre-frontal cortex

This part of the brain:

- co-ordinates the signals from across the cortex / thinking brain;
- is the area responsible for planning and predicting (crucial for lawyers) and, unsurprisingly given this role, it is also implicated in our feelings of frustration and anxiety;[3]
- assesses threats within the sensory information provided by the thalamus (in conjunction with the amygdala – see below);
- does not fully develop until our early 20s;

Traumatic stress, particularly chronic stress or in post-traumatic stress disorder (PTSD), can affect the regulatory ability of the pre-frontal cortex;

Damage to this area can, among other things, make 'temporal' thinking difficult (eg answering questions such as 'in what order did the incident happen?' or 'how long ago was the incident?')

The importance for working in the legal profession of a fully engaged and functioning pre-frontal cortex

Van Der Kolk[4] sets out the following key functions of the pre-frontal cortex which describe some of the key skills of an effective lawyer:

- planning and anticipation;
- sense of time and context;
- inhibition of inappropriate actions;
- empathetic understanding.

Traumatic stress can disengage this executive functioning. In the event of danger, it makes sense that our survival brain takes control.

---

3   For this reason, lobotomies were conducted in the 1940s and 1950s – predominantly on women to 'cure' psychological distress. For a fascinating history of this procedure and the case that informs our modern understanding of memory, read *Patient H.M.: a story of memory, madness, and family secrets* by Luke Dittrich (Random House, 2017).

4   *The body keeps the score: mind, brain, and body in the healing of trauma*, Penguin Random House, 2015, p59.

Survival brain

Limbic system

Beneath the problem-solving cortex, is our 'survival' brain, which contains the parts most closely involved in processing emotion, memory and our basic survival instincts. At its core the brain is a selfish organ focussed on survival at all costs, even if – sometimes – the means of our survival make us feel terrible. Our limbic system reacts before our conscious minds are even aware.

The limbic system is a set of brain structures which includes the amygdala, hippocampus, hypothalamus and (part of the) thalamus.[5]

Thalamus

Sensory input (sight, sound, proprioception, touch, etc) arrives at the thalamus. Its role is to create a coherent moment-by-moment experience of the input.

The thalamus passes this information to:

1) the amygdala (the faster connection and assessment of threat);
2) the pre-frontal cortex (slower but more reliable assessment of threat);
3) sensory information to other relevant areas of the cortex.

It also plays a role in filtering relevant and irrelevant information (for example, you may be conscious of the sound of your colleague speaking in the hallway but – ideally – you are able to filter that out to focus on the task in front of you). In a post-traumatic stress response, this ability is compromised and everything is processed as a potential threat. It is therefore difficult to focus on one particular task as your mind cannot filter out other sensory input which is not relevant.

If the processing of the thalamus is disrupted, it cannot provide a coherent and chronological moment-to-moment experience to the rest of the brain. This is thought to be connected to the experience of flashbacks, which are a feature of post-traumatic stress responses.

---

5 Historically it was considered the centre of emotions in the brain and although modern neuroscientific research has discovered the situation is more complex than this, it is still a helpful structure for our understanding of the issues discussed in this book.

Amygdala

The amygdala:

- is the first part of our body-mind to make an assessment about threats to our survival, and does so quickly;
- acts in conjunction with the hippocampus, which accesses information about relevant past experience;
- sends messages via the autonomic nervous system to make adjustments;
- is a kind of interface between the 'thinking' and 'survival' brains;
- has a role in controlling the sympathetic division (fight/flight) of the autonomic nervous system (explained below);
- is associated with emotions connected to specific memories;
- is a link between the nervous and endocrine systems (see 'allostatic load' below).

Hypothalamus

The hypothalamus:

- is responsible for behavioural drives, and is also associated with emotion;
- sends signals to facial muscles creating involuntary facial expressions (eg rage);
- co-ordinates between the voluntary and autonomic nervous system functions (explained below);
- controls circadian rhythm (the internal body clock);
- sets off communication with the pituitary and adrenal glands, regulating the circulation of stress hormones.

Memory

The hippocampus and amygdala are crucial for memory consolidation. Most long-term memory is stored in the cortex, but shock can stop memories moving from short-term to long-term memory.

Clearly, memory consolidation is hugely important in work, and can make a huge difference in our practice from being reactive on our feet in court or in our time recording in the office. If we feel we are having to look up simple points of law repeatedly, or are working slowly to double-check facts 'unnecessarily', we might consider we are working too slowly and we will either have our time recording slashed at assessment or we will under-record our time to a figure that we think is more reasonable. We might feel the need to work weekends and evenings to 'make up' for this, becoming more stressed and entering into a vicious cycle.

We might also have trouble remembering the details of a conversation with a client if, for example, we had just been exposed to some shocking information or photographs (either in that case or a previous one).

'With burnout . . . I would work myself too hard to keep up with expectations I thought I need to meet. That resulted in becoming more anxious and making myself feel worse . . . It did make me wonder about working in the law and whether I could get through it. I worried about affecting my studies. But, I do not think it was my fault; the pressure put on my role was unrealistic. I have been told that by the other people who were working in my role as well.'

Paralegal (now pupil barrister)

Brain stem

The brain stem regulates the most basic survival functions: hunger, sleep, consciousness, heartbeat, breathing. It links the brain to the rest of the nervous system.

Beyond the brain: the nervous system

The nervous system detects and responds to external and internal stimuli. It comprises two main parts: the *central nervous system* and the *peripheral nervous system*. The most relevant branch for the understanding of trauma is the autonomic nervous system (ANS). The ANS is made up of two further parts: the *sympathetic* (activated to mobilise energy and focus) and *parasympathetic* (activated to restore the body back to its resting state). These final two 'branches' are most relevant to the understanding of stress responses.

Autonomic nervous system

The autonomic nervous system is made up of two divisions: the *sympathetic* nervous system, which signals for the body to be ready for sudden and intense physical activity (sometimes known as the 'accelerator'); and the *parasympathetic* nervous system, which is a resting state which conserves energy and promotes sedentary activity like digestion (the 'brake'). Like an accelerator and a brake, they work in tandem. Although historically understood as 'automatic' systems in modern Western science, in cultures, religions and sciences across global majority societies it has long been understood that the mind-body interplay is more complex. We do have some conscious control over autonomic systems (see Window of Tolerance section).

Sympathetic nervous system

The sympathetic nervous system:

- manages 'fight or flight' – readying for action;
- puts us in an alert state;
- causes increase in blood pressure, heart rate and breathing rate;
- gets us ready to spend energy, linked to risk-taking and a temporary reduction in sensitivity to pain;
- creates increased muscle tone (which may be expressed as a feeling of being tense or shaking/shivering);
- causes a dry mouth;
- restricts peripheral blood vessels (to focus energy on vital functions) and halts digestive tract movement;
- dilates respiratory pathways, making it easier to breathe;
- is activated as we inhale (heart rate increases).

See 'hyper-arousal' in the 'window of tolerance' section below.

Parasympathetic nervous system

The parasympathetic nervous system:

- manages 'feed and breed'; 'rest and digest':
  - salivation;
  - constriction of pupils (allowing better focus on nearby objects);
  - better working of the muscles in the digestive tract;
  - increase of nutrient content in the blood;
  - activated as we exhale (heart rate slows);
- manages 'faint or freeze' – when under stress or after a shock, if the 'fight or flight' sympathetic nervous system response fails, the parasympathetic nervous system kicks in:
  - heart rate is slowed and blood pressure drops;

– the brain's alternative survival mode is activated, and at the extreme end we may faint (a vivid example would be a person with a fear of the sight of blood).

See 'hypo-arousal' in the 'window of tolerance' section below.

Working in tandem

The sympathetic and parasympathetic systems work in tandem, and some organs are connected to (or 'innervated' by) both branches. In these cases, there are the obvious opposing forces of their effects, ie the increase and decrease of heart rate.

Traumatic stress can overwhelm the system. If we are already burnt out and exhausted, we are less likely to be able to regulate ourselves after an experience of trauma.

So, if we are already burnt out and – without much warning or without the time to prepare ourselves – we are exposed to, for example, CCTV footage of a violent incident, we are at higher risk of a post-traumatic stress response and more sensitive to triggers. This is two-directional: if we have experienced acute traumatic stress, we may be more at risk of burnout because of our nervous system already 'working overtime' to stay regulated. This is particularly problematic where we are systematically unprepared and untrained for the trauma presented in any such footage or incident. The feeling that we are so grossly unprepared and untrained for those moments can also be demoralising and stressful.

CW: death in custody

'Similarly with CCTV footage, I know that I am going to have to watch it, that's fine, that's part of the job, but not risk assessing it? There is no assessment of wellbeing around watching distressing material.

This afternoon I was watching a death in custody and someone dying over a long time. There is no check-in, it is just accepted that other people do it, so you need to do it, you need to 'get on'. It is such an outdated view of mental health: if we have done it before then you can do it now, kind of thing.'

Paralegal

Window of tolerance

What is it?

The complex and awe-inspiring systems of our bodies are in a constant dance of interactions known as *allostasis*. When things are working well, these interactions are moving around – and towards – balance: *homeostasis*. The primary systems involved are the autonomic nervous system (as set out above), the endocrine system (which controls hormones) and the immune system.

As discussed above, the protective and adaptive working of our nervous system can be understood as a spectrum of responses with a response that tends towards a 'heightened' nervous system response (hyper-arousal) or a 'deadened' response (hypo-arousal).

The 'spectrum' is helpful in understanding the range of responses, but does not mean that an individual's experience would move smoothly along it, up and down, always passing through the mid-point. It is possible to be in a high state of nervous system arousal and suddenly switch into a hypo-arousal state. It is also possible to experience a swinging back and forth between the two over a relatively short period of time, even within the course of a day. For example, switching between periods of insomnia and periods of excessive sleeping. Each person may tend towards a particular pattern (hyper, hypo or oscillation).

This model can be helpful in understanding our own experience or that of our colleagues. It can also be a useful tool in dealing with states on the spectrum that are extreme enough to affect our quality of life, our ability to work effectively or our health.

A little 'dysregulation' is absolutely normal as part of a fully functioning nervous system. When we are able to pay attention to our own particular patterns of dysregulation, then they can be helpful warning signs that we may need to adjust our course, take some time to rest or make other changes.

A healthy and functioning nervous system moves between states in response to the challenges and needs in the environment. While either extreme on the scale can be debilitating, there is a natural range around the middle of this spectrum which psychologists term 'the window of tolerance'.[6]

---

6 Dr Daniel Siegel.

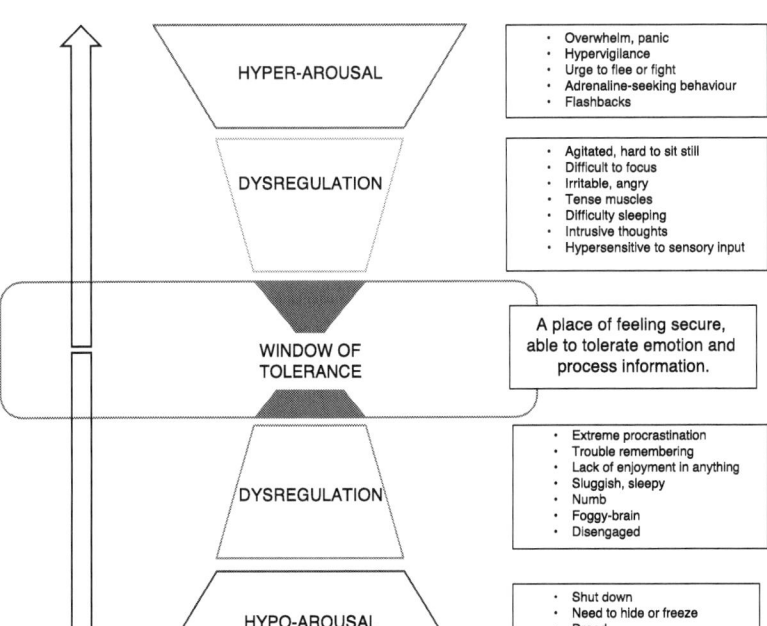

What does it mean in practice?

If we remember that vicarious trauma is normal, even inevitable to some extent, we can focus on bringing awareness to the ways in which it may affect us or those we work with. By understanding it as a protective, survival response, we can hopefully be more compassionate and understanding with ourselves and others.

One of the most pernicious effects of burnout and vicarious trauma can be the extent to which it affects our ability to work as effectively as we are used to. Lawyers, whichever route we have taken or are taking to qualification, will have studied hard, passed numerous assessments and challenging interviews. We may strongly identify with the role – someone who solves problems, has a wealth of knowledge and expertise, can think quickly under pressure, and has attention to detail.

'With burnout, my experience is as a result of the anxiety. I would work myself too hard to keep up with expectations I thought I need to meet. That resulted in becoming more anxious and making myself feel worse.'

Pupil barrister

Chronic stress, burnout and vicarious trauma can affect the functioning of cognitive processes, particularly the pre-frontal cortex (see page 47 above) which directly limits our ability to use these skills.

As described above, the initial stress response may make it easier to focus on a task and get work done to a deadline. We might rely on, or thrive on, this physiological kick. With the right support and structure, this stress response can kick into gear when needed, and then the mind-body can revert back to resting state in order to recover for the next burst of activity.

However, when the mind-body response stays in chronic stress or experiences acute stress or traumatic stress, the effects can be less helpful or actively damaging.

We set out below some of the terms used to describe a particular group of effects (and in some cases, comprise a psychiatric diagnosis). However, for many it might be the case that we experience a range of difficult effects that do not fit any particular category but nonetheless have an effect on our ability to best represent our clients and maintain our quality of life.

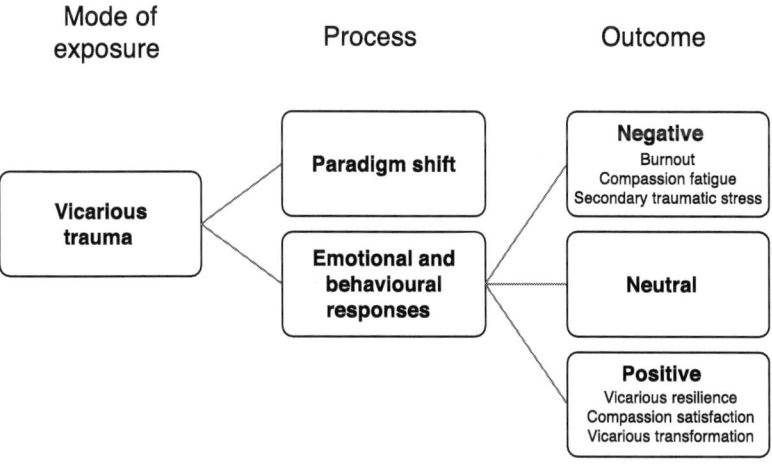

Burnout and compassion fatigue

The following section sets out four different descriptions or categories of negative outcomes: burnout, compassion fatigue, secondary traumatic stress and PTSD. These are not intended to be diagnostic tools or even fixed definitions. Only PTSD is recognised as a psychiatric 'disorder'. Instead, they are offered as useful language and frameworks for our own self-reflection and to normalise these kinds of effects in the legal profession. They must also be considered within the particular context that lawyers are working in (see chapter 7). If you need further support there are a range of resources at appendix B.

Burnout or compassion fatigue are probably some of the most common negative effects of working in legal aid and social welfare law. If we have not experienced it ourselves, it is likely we know a colleague or peer who has. They are both workplace issues that arise out of systemic problems, and are not a sign of personal failing. However, when we have experienced burnout and/or compassion fatigue, we might experience a real loss of confidence and always be worried about it happening again.

It is vital that we get to know our own warning signs, make time and space to take care of ourselves individually and collectively and – as a profession – to push for change.

> 'I don't sometimes realise personally when I am heading towards that situation, so it's more that my response is due to others – usually my family – bringing it to my attention. It is at that point that I will take a step back and ask for some annual leave. Again, it is not something that I personally respond to, it's often others who will say, "I think you need a little break".'
>
> *Solicitor*

Burnout

Burnout describes the mental and physical effects of chronic stress in the workplace. It is a systemic issue often arising out of persistent conflict between the demands placed upon an individual and the resources available to them. Other risk factors include:

- conflict between personal and organisational values;
- lack of control over the quality of work or service provided;

- discrepancy between effort expended and the reward (financial or otherwise);
- unfairness or discord between colleagues.

A lot of stress is due to lack of autonomy. I am at the bottom of the ladder, every choice that is made is not my own. I can suggest things and put forward the way things might happen. I am lucky that my current fee earner listens, but I have worked with previous fee earners who have very different ideas and ways of working . . . you have to constantly look competent. So if you are stressed or burnt out, you feel you have to hide it, as you don't want people to think you are not coping. This is a job that will naturally involve stress. So it's knowing a job is inherently stressful and trying to hide when you're feeling stressed.'

Paralegal

'The effects of burnout are comparable to those of depression, but is more contextual and linked to work (for example, if you leave your job you may feel instant and lasting relief). It might also be understood as a prolonged state of ANS hypo-arousal (see page 52). Effects can include:

- exhaustion;
- other physical symptoms like headaches or digestive issues;
- depression;
- anxiety;
- insomnia;
- self-doubt, helplessness, hopelessness;
- apathy and disillusionment.

It is also considered an 'occupational phenomenon' (not a psychiatric diagnosis) by the World Health Organization 'resulting from chronic workplace stress that has not been successfully managed' which is characterised by:

1) feelings of energy depletion or exhaustion;
2) increased mental distance from one's job or feelings of negativism or cynicism relating to one's job;
3) reduced professional efficacy.[7]

7 *International classification of diseases*, World Health Organization.

> 'In one of the most difficult cases I worked on it was really tricky in terms of getting disclosure from the client about what happened to him. When I was in meetings with him I would sometimes act in a way that, on reflection, didn't focus enough on the client's needs because I'd be getting so wound up. I had deadlines, and the barrister is telling me "we need X, Y and Z" and I couldn't get the information I needed from him. I knew I shouldn't react that way but there were times when I was just so exhausted and stressed that I couldn't give the client the proper client care.'
>
> *Solicitor*

Burnout is a general term and it does not always capture the full experience of lawyers (or other professionals) who work with trauma.

Compassion fatigue

> The emotional and physical fatigue experienced by professionals due to their chronic use of empathy in helping others in distress.[8]

Compassion fatigue is a phenomena within the helping profession, specific to the type of work. It was first used to describe the particular kind of burnout affecting nurses who dealt with traumatic experiences at work.

It can manifest as a loss of compassion towards your clients, your friends and family, or in relation to wider social issues. This can be a particularly alarming shift for those who have chosen their particular line of work and who are motivated by their compassion. Indeed, a person's greater capacity for empathy can increase their risk of compassion fatigue.[9]

---

8 D Turgoose and L Maddox. 'Predictors of compassion fatigue in mental health professionals: a narrative review', *Traumatology*, (2017) 23(2), 172–185: http://dx.doi.org/10.1037/trm0000116.

9 CR Figley, 'Coping with stressors on the home front', *Journal of Social Issues*, 49 (1993), 4, 51–71.

'In legal aid and human rights, you find people who do this work because they care, the sense of injustice burns through them. They are not just working on "a case" but with and for a real person. But they are also competitive and used to high achieving and success. That can become a problem when you can't find a balance.'

Senior caseworker

Sometimes described as 'the cost of caring',[10] the effects can ripple out into relationships with family members and friends. If you have caring responsibilities outside of work, you may be more at risk.

A 2017 review[11] of studies on compassion fatigue in mental health professionals identified several common factors associated with it:

- Most commonly associated with compassion fatigue was a personal experience of traumatic life events.
- A greater level of mindfulness was associated with lower levels of compassion fatigue.
- Increased levels of empathy tended to be related to increased compassion fatigue.
- Perhaps least surprising of all is the link between caseload and compassion fatigue – three studies found a link between higher compassion fatigue and higher numbers of clients / increased time spent with clients.
- There were mixed findings in relation to length of experience in the work. There may be higher levels of compassion fatigue in the junior end of the profession because of inexperience, or lower levels because people are more likely to have dropped out of the profession at an early stage if they experience compassion fatigue. At the other end of the profession, there may be higher rates amongst senior practitioners as they have cumulatively more exposure and are dealing with more complex cases, or their levels may be lower because they have developed better strategies for the longevity of their career.

10 C R Figley (1995). *Compassion fatigue: toward a new understanding of the costs of caring.*

11 D Turgoose and L Maddox. 'Predictors of compassion fatigue in mental health professionals: a narrative review', *Traumatology*, (2017) 23(2), 172–185 http://dx.doi.org/10.1037/trm0000116.

Burnout and compassion fatigue are highly correlated, and high levels of compassion satisfaction (discussed below) are highly correlated with low levels of compassion fatigue.[12] See also the ProQuol measure in appendix A at page 167.

For lawyers

Research into and understanding of compassion fatigue has centred on professions where the empathy is thought to play a key role in the undertaking of the service provided by that professional (ie counsellors, social workers, nurses). This is not generally the case in the legal profession traditionally, and it is not a feature of our training.

However, empathy is not something that we simply 'switch off' as lawyers. Even if lawyers were able to do so, removing an empathetic connection with our clients is not necessarily beneficial for either party. It can help build the relationship of trust necessary to properly represent our clients and – in the context of an empathetic connection – can enable us to experience satisfaction in our work / can enable us to experience compassion satisfaction in our work.

Secondary traumatic stress

Secondary traumatic stress (STS) describes the effects of vicarious, or secondary, trauma that mirror the post-traumatic responses of primary or direct trauma experience.

The response is, at its core, a nervous system response, along two scales (see diagram X):

- hyper-arousal – commonly described as the 'fight or flight' response; and
- hypo-arousal – commonly described as the 'faint or freeze' response.

In the trauma response, these responses may be magnified, and we may feel 'stuck' in one kind of response, or we may oscillate up and down the spectrum.

---

12   D Turgoose and L Maddox. 'Predictors of compassion fatigue in mental health professionals: a narrative review', *Traumatology*, (2017) 23(2), 172–185: http://dx.doi.org/10.1037/trm0000116.

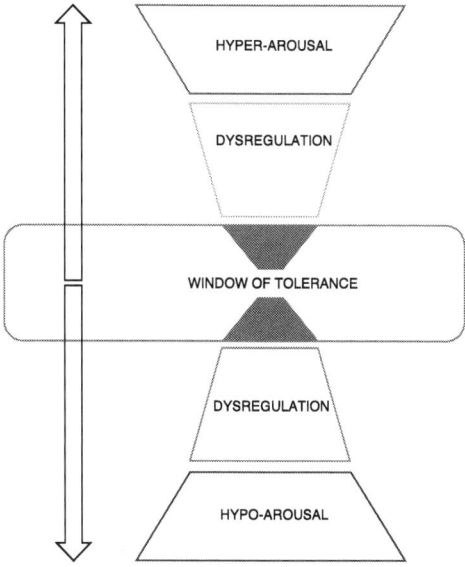

Hyper-arousal

Every individual may experience the effects differently but the following categories might help identify our own responses.

'Flight' response

We might literally flee, but if that is not – or does not feel – possible, we may find that our internal state is preparing us to run even if we physically won't. We might notice a particular tendency to jump from one thing to another, constantly moving, leaving, shifting. It might mean always checking for exits in a room, or constantly planning for a getaway (from a situation, a firm or perhaps the profession as a whole). It could be a feeling of a need to get away even when not in danger, perhaps even leaving situations without really being conscious of why. Another familiar experience might be a feeling of not being able to stop, where taking a break or resting feels unmanageable, impossible or even unsafe.

'Fight' response

This response can be on a scale from an increase in irritability to outbursts of anger or violence. The body is prepared to fight, and so might feel very tense in muscles.

Re-experiencing

Re-experiencing can manifest as:

- not being able to stop thinking about cases;
- staying awake at night running through details of a case;
- at the more extreme end of the scale, this may extend into re-experiencing traumatic moments, or aspects of them, in nightmares or flashbacks;
- feeling teary and upset frequently.

Reactivity

Reactivity can comprise:

- startling easily;
- hypersensitivity, for example to the noise of your colleague's typing or the halogen lighting in court;
- difficulty going to sleep or staying asleep;
- being jumpy;
- difficulty concentrating;
- irritability;
- dread, feeling like something bad is about to happen;
- being unable to filter relevant from non-relevant stimuli, and so everything is perceived as a potential threat (which can lead to behaviours that try to block out other input – ie avoidance).

Cognitive effects of hyper-arousal

Hyper-arousal can have the following cognitive effects:

- disorganised thoughts;
- chaotic thoughts;
- a feeling of too many thoughts, jumping from one to another;
- sense of urgency, even panic, as a default state.

Hypo-arousal

The hypo-arousal range of responses tend to be (although are not necessarily) when the stress is more severe or has been going on for longer. They therefore tend to be more serious warning signs of traumatic stress.

'Freeze' response

We might feel stuck, frozen or paralysed. This might be physical – eg feeling unable to act; or mental – for example not being able to work through thought processes.

'Appease/fawn' response

We may become very skilled at focussing on the needs and demands placed upon us, at the cost of our own needs and our own self-esteem. If, for example, we feel that our safety and survival depends on our ability to attune to the emotions or behaviours of others – particularly whom we depend for survival – then it makes sense that a trauma response might involve appeasement.

'Faint/flop/dissociative' response

We might all have experienced a brief period of dissociation, spacing out for a moment during a client interview or while at your desk. However, the experience can be much more severe, feeling like you have 'lost' long periods of time.

It is, as with all of these responses, a way of the body and mind coping with a distressing experience. Dissociation can happen unconsciously following a triggering event. For some, it can be a conscious choice to dissociate as a coping tool, particularly when faced with chronic trauma or triggering situations.

In a profession where every minute matters (and is often counted), the effect of dissociating can have serious knock-on effects of extra pressure at deadlines, or working longer hours to make up time and meet targets.

Versions of dissociation include depersonalisation (feeling as if you are observing yourself or disconnecting from your body) and derealisation (a sense of the world around you not feeling real).

Avoidance

An avoidant response can consist of:

- feeling numb emotionally;
- lacking motivation about the future: personal, professional or global;
- avoiding socialising;
- lacking interest in the things that are usually enjoyable;
- being less active;
- avoiding anything that might remind you of work;

- avoiding working on particular cases whenever possible;
- forgetfulness, for example being unable to remember parts of a client meeting.

An avoidant response can manifest psychologically or behaviourally, both of which can make legal practice difficult.

> I just couldn't bring myself to go through the papers and I know it was my job to do so. Fortunately I got a silk on that particular case, which was fine, but I do worry if I had not got an extension to the public funding certificate [for a silk], whether I would be able to do that [to go through the material]. I would stop or skim over it – and I know I really needed to know what was in that bundle, in the police bundle, and in the text messages.'
>
> *Barrister*

Psychologically, avoidance may mean forgetfulness where the trauma has prevented long-term memories from being formed. (In some ways, it is the other end of the spectrum from intrusive thoughts – from not being able to stop thinking about something, to not being able to think about it, even when we try to recall it.) It might also manifest in numbness or excessive sleepiness – again, ways of preventing ourselves from engaging with work.

Behaviourally, we may avoid working on particular cases by ignoring telephone calls or emails, putting off chasing up issues on 'that' case, or leave work unnecessarily to the deadline. This may be a tendency on a few cases, or become a widespread and critical problem.

> 'Billing is a prime example for me, I really don't want to revisit the case. I know it's administrative, you just pull out orders, you don't have to revisit the material – it's the psychological revisiting; I just don't want to do it. That really hinders and that causes me lots of stress because I know I should be doing that too.'
>
> *Barrister*

Numbing

A numbing response may consist of:

- hopelessness;
- being unable to enjoy things;
- forgetfulness;
- feeling numb – physically or emotionally;
- trying to block out feelings (eg using substances).

'I think I binge drink as a result of or on the back of finishing a tough case. Most certainly I drink a lot of alcohol or use cocaine – it is kind of a blow-out . . . I go out and drink and decompress . . . I find someone to enable me to go out and get really drunk, which is part of the stress.'

Barrister

Cognitive effects of hypo-arousal

Hypo-arousal can have the following cognitive effects:

- blocked, foggy mind;
- slower thoughts;
- mind going blank when facing difficulty;
- feeling unable to listen.

Physical effects of secondary traumatic stress

There are a variety of physical responses to secondary traumatic stress that may affect our quality of life or our ability to work effectively – for example:

- insomnia;
- disturbance of menstrual cycles, heavier or lighter periods than usual, more painful periods;
- headaches;
- digestive issues;
- reduced immune system functioning;
- chronic pain.

Reasons we may respond differently to secondary traumatic stress

Which are more socially or culturally acceptable responses to stress or trauma – for you? For people you are close to?

For example, is anger and aggression a tolerated response, but not crying or hiding away? Is reduced sleep and working long hours acceptable, but not excess sleeping?

Which kinds of effects do you feel more comfortable discussing with close friends/family/partner? What about with colleagues or a supervisor? Which type of responses (if any) would you seek support for from work or from a medical / mental health professional?

Our different identities, cultures and communities may also influence the acceptability of different responses.

Post-traumatic stress disorder

This book is not designed to diagnose. Regardless of whether you feel you fit the criteria for PTSD or not, if you are experiencing physical, psychological or other difficulties that are affecting your ability to work, or your personal life, then seek help from your GP and let your employer know. If you are self-employed, speak to a trusted peer or let someone in the clerking team or chambers administration know.

You may not consider that you have PTSD, but, depending on your circumstances, receiving a diagnosis of PTSD may give you access to trauma-specific treatment, such as trauma-focussed cognitive behavioural therapy (CBT); eye movement desensitisation and reprocessing (EMDR) therapy; peer support for PTSD; or medication.

Practice: 5-4-3-2-1

Bringing attention to the potential impact of trauma can be tough-going, particularly if we have not had much opportunity to reflect up until now.

If you notice that you are feeling spacey, numb or dissociating, one helpful practice is to use '5-4-3-2-1'.

First, look around the room you are in and count 5 different objects (including behind you and at objects near or far). Then, notice 4 different textures that you can feel. Then, see if you can notice 3 different sounds around you. Then, 2 different smells. Finally, see if you can notice 1 taste.

Drawing attention to the senses can help bring us back to the here and now when it is safe to do so.

CHAPTER 6

Guilt and compassion satisfaction and risk factors

Guilt and doing 'enough'

Guilt can be one of the most insidious effects of vicarious trauma – as not only is it an inherently unpleasant feeling, but it can also silence the very real – and sometimes very harmful – impacts of working with trauma.

For many of us, activism, volunteering or campaigning may invigorate and sustain us, providing a way to stay connected to core values, a shift of gear from day-to-day work, which may be paperwork-heavy, repetitive, etc. It also may be a part of collective self-care.

However, it can sometimes be a way to try to answer the voice that says 'you aren't doing enough, you don't deserve the nice home or the safety that you have'.

'It is so hard to have a good work/life balance when you work in civil liberties / human rights areas. You almost feel like you have to be fighting every battle that is out there. You are trying to fight the battle with work, then you go on Twitter and there are 10 more things to be upset and enraged about and so you are trying to deal with all of those things too.

It is never ending, the number of issues you can engage with and try to contribute to . . . which is a very depressing way of dealing with things. You are trying to deal with things at work, but it is difficult if you try to switch off . . .'

Paralegal

'There seems to be an automatic assumption that if you are in the field you can handle it. So it's kind of this perception of weakness, or not being as good in your job as others who don't complain, so it then sometimes silences you because of that perception.'

Solicitor

Guilt is thought to be one of the causal mechanisms in the development of post-traumatic stress[1] – and reducing feelings of guilt and fear can assist positive recovery and growth after trauma.[2]

At its worst, it is also a way for employers and colleagues to disempower staff or resist efforts to change the workplace culture. This can have a profound and pernicious effect.

To be clear: we readily accept that legal aid and social welfare law is an extraordinary and humbling field to work in. Often we are working in service of clients whose strength can be deeply affecting. We may be working on strategic legal challenges that have the power to bring about change for multiple marginalised persons or groups at once.

However, the privilege of undertaking this work must not be used as a catch-all to smother practitioner experience of vicarious trauma, burnout, stress or otherwise. This work can be relentlessly tough and desperately upsetting; it can and does leave a mark. The freedom and permission to discuss the impact of our work is critical to our survival in the profession and to the proper and safe service of our clients' best interests.

'There are a whole host of issues at the starting end too: how poorly treated you are, the culture of superiority and combined with that, this culture of not allowing yourself to acknowledge that it's really hard. You are treated as though you are seeing yourself as some kind of martyr if you moan about it. I remember saying to a colleague that I was finding it hard and they dismissed me, comparing my situation to what our clients were going through. But the two are not mutually exclusive. You should be allowed to say that things are difficult.'

Solicitor

---

1 Konstantin Bub and Miriam JJ Lommen, 'The role of guilt in posttraumatic stress disorder', *European Journal of Psychotraumatology*, (2017) 8:1, 1407202, DOI: 10.1080/20008198.2017.1407202.

2 Wenchao Wang, Xinchun Wu and Xiaoyu Lan, 'Rumination mediates the relationships of fear and guilt to posttraumatic stress disorder and posttraumatic growth among adolescents after the Ya'an earthquake', *European Journal of Psychotraumatology*, (2020) 11:1, 1704993, DOI: 10.1080/20008198.2019.1704993.

Compassion satisfaction and vicarious resilience

Given the limited attention paid within the legal sector to dealing with trauma in a professional setting, this book is focussed on negative effects of working with trauma. However, those of us who work with clients who have experienced tremendous tragedy, oppression and discrimination will instinctively know that there is another side to this coin: *compassion satisfaction*, ie the great satisfaction of such work; and *vicarious resilience*, ie the vicarious strength and resilience we may feel from seeing our clients survive and thrive.

There has been very little research into these issues in relation to the legal profession. However, the factors we have set out throughout this book that can reduce the negative effects of vicarious trauma can can also contribute to the positive effects of working with trauma, and vice versa.[3]

How can we measure them?

There are several questionnaires that are used by clinicians to assess or diagnose, or by academics for research.

One useful measure that captures a variety of experiences and effects is the Professional Quality of Life (ProQOL) scale.[4] The ProQOL is a self-score questionnaire that measures compassion satisfaction (and compassion fatigue). It is designed for those who are exposed to potentially traumatising material as a result of paid or volunteer work. (See also the sections above on burnout and compassion fatigue; and secondary traumatic stress.)

It is not designed to provide any kind of clinical diagnosis. It can be a useful tool for self-reflection, or as a tool to bring information to supervision. It could also be used on an anonymous basis at an organisational level to measure the overall levels in an organisation.

The full ProQOL scale is included in appendix A at page 167.

---

3   M Pack, 'Clinical supervision, the use of support, humour, spirituality, and ongoing training were variables identified by the participants as ameliorating vicarious traumatization', 2014; 'Vicarious resilience: a multilayered model of stress and trauma', Affilia: Journal of Women & Social Work, *29*(1), 18–29; https://doi.org/10.1177/0886109913510088.

4   © B. Hudnall Stamm, 2009–2012. 'Professional Quality of Life: Compassion Satisfaction and Fatigue Version 5 (ProQOL)': www.proqol.org. This test may be freely copied as long as (a) author is credited, (b) no changes are made, and (c) it is not sold. Those interested in using the test should visit www.proqol.org to verify that the copy they are using is the most current version of the test. This measure is available for free in multiple languages on the website.

Risk factors: what puts us at risk?

When we consider the risk factors, our baseline is that vicarious trauma, compassion fatigue and burnout are occupational hazards and not personal failings.

There are risk factors at an individual level and at a group and organisational level:

- individual:
  - ☐ individual differences;
  - ☐ personal history of trauma / systemic or ongoing trauma;
  - ☐ coping styles;
- team / organisation / collective:
  - ☐ workplace support (peer support);
  - ☐ caseload;
  - ☐ supervision.

Individual risk factors

Individual personality traits

There is a wealth of research into differences in personality traits and how they interact with mental health outcomes. Most are carried out by self-report questionnaires (the Myers-Briggs test being a famous example[5]). Other research uses twin studies to examine hereditability of our personality, and there has also been some exploration at a neurological level.[6]

Personality traits are considered to some extent fixed aspects of ourselves, and longitudinal research has found that they tend to be stable over time.[7] However, particular traits are not determinative or wholly predictive of how we will respond to any given situation. There is no unified view on the relative influence of genetics and environment, or how changeable they might be over time.[8]

Much research on the individual differences of personality traits in psychology revolves around the 'five factors'[9] also known as the

5 See: www.myersbriggs.org/my-mbti-personality-type/mbti-basics/.
6 J Maltby, L Day and A Macaskill, *Personality, individual differences and intelligence*, Pearson Education, 2010.
7 EK Graham, SJ Weston, D Gerstorf, TB Yoneda, T Booth, CR Beam, R Estabrook (2020) 'Trajectories of Big Five Personality Traits: a coordinated analysis of 16 longitudinal samples' *European Journal of Personality*.
8 PT Costa and RR McCrae (1992), 'Normal personality assessment in clinical practice: The NEO Personality Inventory', Psychological assessment, 4(1), 5.
9 Costa and McCrae, 1992.

'Big Five'. There is of course debate about the extent to which these five factors are able to account for all variations of personality, but they do have a large body of research behind them and so are useful to understand in order to understand the research.

Each factor describes a sliding scale, where we each tend to fall somewhere along the continuum.

The 'Big Five' are:

HIGH	LOW
Openness	
Willingness to consider new ideas, have new experiences	Conventional, prefer the familiar to the new
Conscientiousness	
Self-control and discipline	Easily distracted, careless
Extraversion	
Sociability	Reserved
Agreeableness	
Sympathetic, altruistic, trusting	Suspicious, sceptical, unco-operative
Neuroticism	
Volatile emotions, anxious	Emotional stability

There are two questions that follow. First, what links are there between personality type and risk of more negative reaction to working with trauma? Second, is there a 'lawyer type' (or even a 'legal aid lawyer type') of personality and what might that tell us about the risks of burnout and vicarious trauma?

The first question has been investigated to some extent. Very broadly, high levels of neuroticism[10] (including, in one study,

---

10 Stavanović et al (2016); Michael Weinberg and Sharon Gil (2016) 'Trauma as an objective or subjective experience: The association between types of traumatic events, personality traits, subjective experience of the event, and posttraumatic symptoms', *Journal of Loss and Trauma*, 21:2, 137–146, DOI: 10.1080/15325024.2015.1011986

lawyers[11]) and low levels of extraversion[12] have been associated with negative trauma reactions.

The second question is less well-researched and perhaps is not answerable. However, we might want to reflect on the personality traits that are commonly valued and upheld in the legal profession, and in the legal aid, social justice and client-centred sectors and consider how they interact with the risks of vicarious trauma (or risks of working in this sector).

We may instinctively recognise ourselves in some of the traits above (or even want to take a test online) and find it a useful way to understand our own risk factors and tendencies. It is also possible to recognise aspects of our personality that are perhaps exacerbated in times of stress or burnout.

Focusing solely on personality traits can reinforce the cultures and messages within the legal profession that blame individuals and make space only for a certain 'type' of person to be successful. While individual differences are useful in understanding the broad range of experiences lawyers may have in response to the work, there are very necessary limits placed on its utility. Personality trait research has a long problematic association with eugenicist views which are racist, classist, ableist, sexist, and violently discriminatory. There is certainly not one 'type' of person who can succeed in the profession and there is far more that *can* be done to change the culture of the legal profession to create environments in which burnout, chronic stress and vicarious trauma are not encouraged to thrive.

11 Grace Maguire and Mitchell K. Byrne (2017) 'The law is not as blind as it seems: relative rates of vicarious trauma among lawyers and mental health professionals', *Psychiatry, Psychology and Law*, 24:2, 233–243, DOI: 10.1080/13218719.2016.1220037.

12 Aleksandra Stevanović, Tanja Frančišković and Eric Vermetten (2016) 'Relationship of early-life trauma, war-related trauma, personality traits, and PTSD symptom severity: a retrospective study on female civilian victims of war', *European Journal of Psychotraumatology*, 7:1, DOI: 10.3402/ejpt.v7.30964

'Unfortunately, I did experience burnout, whilst working at one firm, but the way I worked combined with the culture across a few firms, is what I believe led to burnout. My body was responding really badly to long hours and a lack of support. It was hard for me to get the support I needed even on a personal level as none of my family or my partner lived near me. I had been a really, really good legal representative for the 4 or 5 years leading up to that. My CV spoke for itself, my achievements too. I felt that the culture at the particular firm when burnout came on meant that I could not ask for the help I needed to stop the burnout becoming a long-term issue.'

Senior caseworker

Mindfulness, grounding and space for pause

One part of 'trait' research in psychology and mental health more generally, which has had its fair share (and more) of attention, is the association between mindfulness and wellbeing. There is a growing 'mindfulness in law' movement in the UK as well as across the globe, from Harvard Law School to the Mindfulness in Law initiative.[13]

Mindfulness usually refers to either:

1) a practice to cultivate attention, non-judgmentally, of the present moment;[14] or

2) a personality trait, sometimes described as dispositional mindfulness, ie 'natural' levels of mindfulness day-to-day.

Research suggests that mindfulness training and practice leads to increased levels of dispositional mindfulness over time. This may be through formal study in meditation within religious practice, informal and secular practice, or formal training through a Mindfulness-Based Intervention ("MBI") (examples below).

There is also evidence that mindfulness and related practices may be beneficial in the context of vicarious trauma, as set out below.

13 See: https://twitter.com/lawmindfulness

14 There is a wide variety of mindfulness-based interventions with rigorous academic research supporting their efficacy, including mindfulness-based cognitive therapy (MBCT) (developed as a treatment for recurrent depression); mindfulness-based stress reduction (MBSR) (for chronic stress and pain); and acceptance and commitment therapy (ACT) (which has particular efficiency for trauma).

In the mind

As lawyers, we live day-to-day in our problem-solving brain (predominantly in the pre-frontal cortex).

This mode of mind helps us reason through tricky problems, plan our day, assess risk, work towards a goal and make judgments. It acts as a 'discrepancy monitor', asking:

- Is this working?
- Should I change this to improve it?
- Do I like it or dislike it?
- How do I get from A to B?

In this mode, our brains become focussed on solving problems. We analyse risk, plan, and run 'what if' scenarios, in an attempt to get to grips with a problem.

As lawyers, these are prized abilities. We are trained throughout our academic study, vocational training and day-to-day practice to value and promote this mode of mind. It is likely to become our habitual mode. Perhaps we notice this when we apply our professional analysis or attention to detail in disagreements in our personal lives. We may try to find solutions to situations in our life that cannot be solved by reasoning, or fixate on judging experiences that cannot be changed and that must, for the moment, be endured.

This problem-solving mind is known to lead to an increase in *rumination*, which is a key mechanism of many mental health difficulties including depression, anxiety and post-traumatic stress.

In the body

Stress can worsen some health conditions and chronic pain. Our body might feel like an unpleasant or even intolerable place to be, so we block out the feeling or try to push it away. It could even happen subconsciously, leaving our bodies feeling numb or disconnected.

Alternatively, we might become acutely aware of every sensation in our body. For example, if we notice a twinge in our back we start to 'problem-solve' and tell stories about the pain, fixating on it.

As we have set out, trauma effects often manifest in the body. To get to know how the work is affecting us, it is helpful to know what is happening in our own bodies. Practices such as mindfulness help to get us in the habit of paying attention to the internal experience of our body in the present moment, in a kind of non-judgmental way. In traditional talking therapies, the focus is on thoughts, feelings and behaviours (eg in Cognitive behavioural therapy (CBT)) but mindfulness explicitly includes paying attention to the body. As trauma is a body-based phenomena, then that seems helpful.

In some ways, mindfulness practice simply helps rebalance the habits of the mind from being exclusively a problem-solving machine to something more flexible that is able to notice and feel our whole moment-to-moment experience.

Research

There is a large body of research that supports mindfulness as a helpful trait and mindfulness practices as helpful interventions for a wide range of issues, including burnout and traumatic stress responses. Research has found that increased levels of mindfulness:

- are predictive of lower traumatic stress symptoms[15] (specifically the ability to accept thoughts and experiences without judgment[16]);
- reduce the link between trauma and symptoms of depression and anxiety;[17]
- are associated with the ability to 'observe one's thoughts and feelings as temporary, objective events in the mind, as opposed to reflections of the self that are necessarily true'[18] (also known as

15   BA Chopko and RC Schwartz (2013) 'The relation between mindfulness and posttraumatic stress symptoms among police officers", *Journal of Loss and Trauma*, 18(1), 1–9. https://doi.org/10.1080/15325024.2012.674442 ; CE Martin, BA Bartlett, MK Reddy, A Gonzalez and AA Vujanovic (2018), Associations between Mindfulness Facets and PTSD Symptom Severity in Psychiatric Inpatients; I Setti and P Argentero (2014), 'The role of mindfulness in protecting firefighters from psychosomatic malaise', *Traumatology*, 20(2), 134–141. https://doi.org/10.1037/h0099398/.

16   Acceptance in the context of mindfulness does *not* mean being passive or being tolerant of wrongdoing, rather it is about accepting the present moment as it is (and not that we cannot change the future).

17   EB Kroska, ML Miller, AI Roche, SK Kroska, MW O'Hara, (2018) 'Effects of traumatic experiences on obsessive-compulsive and internalizing symptoms: the role of avoidance and mindfulness', *Journal of Affective Disorders*, 225 (April 2017), 326–336. https://doi.org/10.1016/j.jad.2017.08.039; CE Martin, BA Bartlett, MK Reddy, A Gonzalez, AA Vujanovic (2018), Associations between Mindfulness Facets and PTSD Symptom Severity in Psychiatric Inpatients; KS Kalill, M Treanor, L Roemer (2014) 'The importance of non-reactivity to posttraumatic stress symptoms: a case for mindfulness'. *Mindfulness*, 5(3), 314–321. https://doi.org/10.1007/s12671-012-0182-6.

18   DM Fresco, MT Moore, MHM van Dulmen, ZV Segal, SH Ma, JD Teasdale, JMG Williams (2007) 'Initial psychometric properties of the experiences questionnaire: validation of a self-report measure of decentering', *Behavior Therapy*, 38(3), 234–246. https://doi.org/10.1016/j.beth.2006.08.003

'decentering') and is linked to reductions in anxiety[19] and the facilitation of post-traumatic growth;[20]

- are associated with decreased 'mind-wandering' away from the task in hand. This is helpful for concentration, of course, but there is also evidence that – as described by the title of one study – 'a wandering mind is an unhappy mind'[21] – for example, mind-wandering can lead to increased rumination on difficult thoughts or feelings (associated with anxiety, depression and post-traumatic stress responses).

The ability to distance one's reactions to feelings, and understand them as a temporary phenomenon in the mind could build resilience against the development of secondary traumatic stress which, by its nature, is exacerbated by cognitive and physiological reactions (eg intrusive thoughts and increased heart rate) in response to events that did not happen directly to the individual.

Research supports the benefits of mindfulness at a physiological level, and participation in MBIs has been found to be associated with reduction in inflammatory biomarkers of stress and post-traumatic stress.[22] Further, there is a growing evidence base through experimental designs that shows that mindfulness interventions are helpful for trauma symptoms from both primary and secondary trauma exposure.[23]

19 EA Hoge, E Bui, E Goetter, DM Fresco and NM Simon (2015) 'Change in Decentering Mediates Improvement in Anxiety in Mindfulness-Based Stress Reduction for Generalized Anxiety Disorder', 228–235. https://doi.org/10.1007/s10608-014-9646-4/.

20 RG Tedeschi and CL Blevins (2015) 'From Mindfulness to Meaning: Implications for the Theory of Posttraumatic Growth' *Psychological Inquiry*, 26(4), 373–376. https://doi.org/10.1080/1047840X.2015.1075354/.

21 Matthew A Killingsworth and Daniel T Gilbert, 'A wandering mind is an unhappy mind', *Science*: www.sciencemag.org/cgi/content/full/330/6006/932/DC1.

22 AM Gallegos, MC Lytle, JA Moynihan and N L Talbot, 'Mindfulness-based stress reduction to enhance psychological functioning and improve inflammatory biomarkers in trauma-exposed women: A pilot study', *Psychological Trauma: Theory, Research, Practice, and Policy*, (2015) 7(6), 525–532; https://doi.org/10.1037/tra0000053.

23 L Hilton, AR Maher, B Colaiaco, E Apaydin, ME Sorbero, M Booth, S Hempel (2016) 'Meditation for Posttraumatic Stress: Systematic Review and Meta-analysis', *Psychological Trauma: Theory, Research, Practice, and Policy*, 9(4), No Pagination Specified. https://doi.org/10.1037/tra0000180; S Slatyer, M Craigie, C Rees, S Davis, T Dolan, D Hegney (2017) 'Nurse Experience of Participation in a Mindfulness-Based Self-Care and Resiliency Intervention', Mindfulness. https://doi.org/10.1007/s12671-017-0802-2/.

Practices that allow us to be mindful of our current state (whether that is a formal seated meditation or an activity that brings us back to the present moment) can help us notice when we have moved outside our 'window of tolerance'.

Although mindfulness practices are not necessarily religious ones, they can be. Prayer, religious ritual and ceremony, chanting, non-religious spiritual practices – all may be practices of mindfulness. Equally, the quality of mindfulness can be applied to non-spiritual practices.

Limitations

It is important to note that behind the hype around mindfulness there is some valid criticism:

- Mindfulness practices have their roots in both ancient and contemporary cultures, particularly in Asia. However, it is often stripped of these connections when packaged and sold in workplaces. There is unfortunately widespread cultural appropriation of these teachings.
- It is not, and should not be treated as, a panacea.
- It is frequently co-opted as a tool of neo-capitalism.[24] We do not include mindfulness, or any other recommend practice here on the basis that it produces more effective tools of capitalism.
- Anything that is powerful enough to have an effect is powerful enough to have a negative as well as positive effect. It is not about relaxation or emptying the mind of thoughts. It is about seeing clearly what is there in the moment. If, in the moment, there is terror, feeling unsafe, hearing distressing voices, seeing violent images and flashbacks, then practicing mindfulness may be worse than inappropriate and may be actively harmful.[25]
- The Pali and Sanskrit languages from which Western scholars translated the words that became 'mindfulness' in English are both sacred languages of religious or spiritual texts.

Personal experience of trauma

As explored above, best estimates are that around a third of UK adults have experienced at least one traumatic event and one in 20 experience symptoms consistent with a PTSD diagnosis. It is intuitive (and

---

24 See, for example: Ron Purser, *McMindfulness: How mindfulness became the new capitalist spirituality*, Repeater Books, 2019.

25 David Treleaven, *Trauma-sensitive mindfulness: Practices for safe and transformative healing*, WW Norton & Company, 2018.

also backed up by the research) that there is a higher risk of the negative effects of workplace exposure to trauma.[26]

An Australia study[27] compared criminal lawyers (who are exposed to trauma) and lawyers working with little to no exposure to trauma. Across the groups, trauma history was associated with higher vicarious trauma measures.

It is important to remember that these studies comment only on populations, rather than individuals. If a person has survived trauma and developed effective strategies to reflect and take care of themselves, then they may be at lower risk.

It may be that there is a particular kind of case that affects you most strongly. This could be connected to personal experience of the kind of incident. However, it is certainly not the case that it is always that way – it may be that working on cases that have personal resonance for you gives you a sense of agency and power.

In this sense it may depend on the outcome, or perceived success of the case (either by you individually or the client or both).

Coping styles

In addition to variance of personality traits predicting levels of secondary traumatic stress, behavioural and cognitive styles of coping with workplace stress are also likely to affect levels of traumatic stress symptoms. Our 'coping styles' are how we respond to stress behaviourally and cognitively.

In psychological study, coping styles are often grouped into two:

1) approach coping – where we go 'towards' the issue to tackle it;
2) avoidance coping – where we move away from it or try to block it out.

26 ME Leclerc, J Wemmers, A Brunet (2020) 'The unseen cost of justice: post-traumatic stress symptoms in Canadian lawyers', *Psychology, Crime & Law*, 26:1, 1-21, DOI: 10.1080/1068316X.2019.1611830, citing: C Brewin, B Andrews and J Valentine (2000) 'Meta-analysis of risk factors for posttraumatic stress disorder in trauma-exposed adults', *Journal of Consulting and Clinical Psychology*, 68(5), 748–766. doi: 10.1037//0022-006X.68.5.748; E Ozer, S Best, T Lipsey, D Weiss (2003) 'Predictors of posttraumatic stress disorder and symptoms in adults: A meta-analysis', *Psychological Bulletin*, 129(1), 52–73. doi: 10.1037/0033-2909.129.1.52

27 PL Vrklevski, J Franklin (2008) 'Vicarious trauma: the impact on solicitors of exposure to traumatic material', *Traumatology*, 14(1), 106–118. https://doi.org/10.1177/1534765607309961/.

However, the literature is mixed and a variety of measures and models have been used in examining these relationships. Difficulties in reviewing the literature arise from the sheer variety in types of possible coping styles and the lack of longitudinal or experimental design research.

Research suggests (but is by no means conclusive) that post-traumatic stress responses are linked to avoidant and 'suppression' coping styles.[28] PTSD could be considered a failure to cope with traumatic thoughts via an inefficient coping style and/or that suppression leads to an incomplete processing of the disturbing stimuli of the traumatic event. It has been suggested that avoidant coping mechanisms may partially account for the mechanism by which dissociation after a traumatic incident progressed to persistent post-traumatic stress.[29]

However, the link is not straightforward – for instance in one study (of a non-clinical population) no link was found between avoidant coping styles and avoidance-type PTSD symptoms.

Furthermore, although it is tempting to consider some coping styles as preferable to others, a study that examined 285 social workers dealing with client suicidal behaviour found that higher levels of secondary traumatic stress were predictive of increased supposedly positive *and* negative coping styles.[30]

It is not uncommon for lawyers to use humour, particularly between colleagues, as a coping style. Interestingly, a 2015 study found that humour was a useful coping tool for workers in a child abuse task force, up to a point. When the humour became darker, and at the expense of victims, this was a 'red flag' for high levels of secondary traumatic stress.[31] Other research has found use of humour as a coping style with secondary trauma signs.[32]

28 M Amir (1997) 'Coping in Post-Traumatic (PTSD)' *Patients Stress Disorder*, 23(3).

29 30 ML Pacella, L Irish, SA Ostrowski, E Sledjeski, JA Ciesla, JW Fallon, DI Delahanty (2011). 'Avoidant coping as a mediator between peritraumatic dissociation and posttraumatic stress disorder symptoms' *Journal of Traumatic Stress*, 24(3), 317-325.

30 31 L Ting, JM Jacobson, S Sanders (2005). *Available Supports and Coping Behaviors of Mental Health Social Workers Following Fatal and Nonfatal Client Suicidal Behavior*, 211–222..

31 32 SW Craun, ML Bourke (2015) Is Laughing at the Expense of Victims and Offenders a Red Flag ? Humor and Secondary Traumatic Stress, (December 2014), 592–602. https://doi.org/10.1080/10538712.2015.1042187

32 33 ML Bourke, SW Craun (2014). Coping With Secondary Traumatic Stress: Differences Between UK and US Child Exploitation Personnel, 20(1), 57–64.

'The office has quite a jokey atmosphere, which is nice, but it's also a case of, "we are all getting on with it". There is no mechanism if I had to bring up stress – I have to bring that up myself.'

Paralegal

In the second half of the book we set out ways in which we can consider our own current coping styles. We will likely have a whole range of them which we rely on in different ways and to different extents. We will consider what role they play in our own personal 'toolkit', and consider how we might add to this toolkit.

Workplace support, caseloads and supervision

The role of workplace support is crucial given lawyers' (and other staff's) duty of confidentiality. The workplace is the only ethically secure space where facts of a case can be named and clients discussed openly.

There are several key organisational factors which research suggests play an important role in addressing vicarious trauma:

- organisational satisfaction;[33]
- supervisor support;[34]
- peer support;
- caseload;
- availability of supervision;
- trauma training.

Unfortunately there is evidence that lawyers working with vulnerable clients are less likely to be offered support from their workplace.[35]

Self-employed barristers, beyond the pupillage relationship, may have their own structures to a greater or lesser extent within chambers or across peer groups or across Inns of Court. This can take the form of continued informal mentoring relationships beyond pupillage, formal mentoring or buddying systems, peer support groups,

---

33 34 BE Perron, BS Hiltz (2006) 'Burnout and secondary trauma among forensic interviewers of abused children', *Child and Adolescent Social Work Journal*, 23(2), 216–234. https://doi.org/10.1007/s10560-005-0044-3/.

34 35 MISSING FOOTNOTE TO FOLLOW

35 Law Society. (2018). *Resilience and wellbeing survey report: Junior Lawyers Division*. London, UK

and wellness or wellbeing policies or initiatives, for example those championed by Wellbeing at the Bar programme, co-founded by Rachel Spearing.[36]

In the solicitor and legal executive side of the profession, supervision may be regular and thorough, or intermittent. It is usually focussed on legal and procedural casework issues.

'You do have supervisions where you are asked how you are finding your workload, but it is very much about volume not the type of work or if there is another problem going on.'

Paralegal

Ethical and professional duties

In order to make meaningful widespread change to the profession, movement needs to come both from the 'bottom' at the level of the individual, but also – we strongly contend – from the 'top'. We work in regulated professions with ethical and conduct rules. There are a number of rules across the professions that should guide us to take better account of the risks of vicarious trauma and related issues, and the effects it can have on our ability to competently carry out our roles.

Professional codes of conduct

Solicitors[37]

3.3 You maintain your competence to carry out your role and keep your professional knowledge and skills up to date.
3.4 You consider and take account of your client's attributes, needs and circumstances.

---

36   See: www.wellbeingatthebar.org.uk.
37   *Solicitors Regulation Authority (SRA) Code of Conduct for Solicitors, RELs and RFLs*, 2019: www.sra.org.uk/solicitors/standards-regulations/code-conduct-solicitors/.

Barristers[38]

CD7 You must provide a competent standard of work and service to each client.

CD10 You must take reasonable steps to manage your practice, or carry out your role within your practice, competently and in such a way as to achieve compliance with your legal and regulatory obligations.

CILEx members and practitioners[39]

You must:

2. Maintain high standards of professional and personal conduct and justify public trust in you, your profession and the provision of legal services.

5. Act competently, in the best interests of your client and respect client confidentiality.

There are no specific guidelines for any of the professions as to how best deal with these issues. However, there are some comparable guidelines which may offer a useful direction.

Special youth proceedings competencies were introduced by the BSB after their review in 2015 raised concerns about the quality of representation of vulnerable young people.[40] Barristers working in the youth court system must declare to the BSB that they have the specialist skills, knowledge and attributes necessary to work effectively with young people, as set out in the competencies and guidance.

Barristers must also have: knowledge and understanding of the additional vulnerabilities of these clients (2.1); recognise vulnerabilities (2.2); adapt the delivery of their service accordingly (2.3). They should also: be alert to particular needs, including mental health needs of a young person (3.1); recognise the difficulties of young

38 *The Bar Standards Board (BSB) Handbook*, 2020: www.barstandardsboard.org.uk/the-bsb-handbook.html.

39 *Code of Conduct of the Chartered Institute of Legal Executives (CILEx) and its regulatory body*, CILEx Regulation: www.cilex.org.uk/about_cilex/about-cilex-lawyers/what-cilex-lawyers-do/code-of-conduct.

40 *Youth Proceedings competences*, BSB, 2017: www.barstandardsboard.org.uk/uploads/assets/197b7604-ac56-4175-b09476ec43ef188c/bsbyouthcompetencies2017forwebsite.pdf.

people engaging with them or other professionals (4.2); have the ability to underhand and build trust with young people (4.3.1); and, engage with relevant organisations to help support their clients (55.2). Such guidance could serve as a precedent for a similar scheme for lawyers working with trauma. The Advocates' Gateway[41], which provides free access to practical, evidence-based guidance on vulnerable witness and defendants, and the Vulnerable Witness Advocacy Training,[42] provide further examples of this approach.

In recent years there have been a number of high-profile disciplinary cases of junior solicitors who have referred to difficult or even toxic working environments combined with mental health struggles.[43] While vicarious trauma was not named as a specific factor, these cases should serve as a warning of the risk to individual careers and the reputation of the professions.

This is a critical moment for the regulators to take active steps to protect and promote staff wellbeing. We urge all regulators to reflect on the evidence collated in this text, which sounds a clarion call for a wholesale reconsideration of education, training and regulation of lawyers working with traumatic caseloads. We also encourage other relevant bodies, including the Legal Aid Agency and Office of the Immigration Services Commissioner to consider these issues in their accreditation and/or contracting policies.

41 https://www.theadvocatesgateway.org
42 https://www.icca.ac.uk/advocacy-the-vulnerable-crime/
43 M Walters, 'Juniors demand answers from SRA on protection from "toxic" work environments', *The Law Society Gazette*, 13 February 2019: www.lawgazette. co.uk/juniors-demand-answers-from-sra-on-protection-from-toxic-work-environments/5069264.article.

CHAPTER 7

The front line: personal, social and political contexts

While considerable academic study and research is focused upon the impact of traumatic workloads – both the process of bearing witness to individual client trauma and the structural traumatisation of vulnerable clients by state systems – much less attention is given to the *structural pressures* within which legal aid and social justice lawyers work day-to-day.

Those pressures matter: they have the power to erode practitioners' motivation, drive and commitment to do their work. This has a direct bearing on access to justice. Practitioner fatigue, apathy, and despair can quickly build when faced with multiple pressures and hostilities. Longer term, these pressures can quite literally wear or burn practitioners out – whether for short periods, or out of the profession completely.

We contend that the structural pressures on lawyers working with vulnerable populations extend – but are not limited – to:

- education;
- training;
- remuneration;
- legal aid funding.

These various pressures should be looked at individually and cumulatively, both in their interaction and effect. Each factor or pressure serves to aggravate and exacerbate the impact of traumatic work, particularly where they come to bear on lawyers, who are themselves human beings. What we mean by this is that each of us bring to work – knowingly or otherwise – the highs and lows, traumas and triumphs, of ordinary life. Many of us also bring a deep-seated internal motivation or drive to do this type of work, which can make us both more and less susceptible to burn out.[1]

CW: suicide

'I think I have had times when the work has stressed me out. I was for a time on medication for depression . . . Also when my colleague took her own life it hit me a lot, she was a close friend to me as well, and we attempted to guide her, and we thought we had got her through it.'

Clerk

---

1 Figley, 2003.

Personal motivations: where do we begin?

Understanding system impact requires an analysis of why practitioners come to this work in the first place.

The personal motivations that draw lawyers to work with vulnerable populations are often dynamic, changing over time as work experience, client experience and life experience come to bear. However, in answer to our question to interviewees about what brought them into the profession, some key themes emerged:

- helping people to navigate unfamiliar legal systems;
- helping people to achieve equality before the law;
- enabling people to have a voice, to be heard, and to be understood;
- an overriding commitment to social justice.

'I had a feeling of social responsibility and wanting to do something with the good degree I had. It's not that I had a terrible background but I had definitely been given the chance to progress and I wanted to use that for good effect.'

Solicitor

'I come from a background of activists. I am a second-generation immigrant from apartheid South Africa. My Dad's family emigrated because of a racially prejudiced regime. On my mother's side they were all political activists too. I wanted to address injustice and inequality.'

Solicitor

'[I wanted] to help individual people who are either having to navigate some area of law – for example inquest law – that they have never navigated before, or to assist people who are vulnerable, struggling or marginalised, or are simply struggling because they are bereaved. It's about helping those people navigate the law in the very difficult situation in which they have found themselves in.'

Paralegal

> 'A strong commitment to social justice. My belief in equality before the law. My desire to assist people who are unable to articulate or maybe even see their own stories.'
>
> *Barrister*
>
> 'Broadly speaking it was a strong sense of the importance of social justice. I had an interest in human rights through campaign work but felt that active legal practice was a better way to ensure rights were respected and protected.'
>
> *Solicitor*

Revisiting and developing these core motivations is cited as a protective factor for practitioners and a sustaining part of working in the field.[2]

It is not uncommon for lawyers to have deeply personal motivations, because they have experienced trauma themselves, either interpersonal trauma or systemic trauma. Often those practitioners want to use their experience in service of other vulnerable, marginalised or traumatised individuals.

> 'It stems from personal experience within my family . . . when I thought about the area of law I wanted to do, I was initially thinking family law, but then I came across the idea that I could do what I wanted to do in family in immigration . . . domestic violence cases or any cases with any particular vulnerability . . . it was tapping into that personal experience and assisting people who might not know how to deal with those difficult situations.'
>
> *Solicitor*

This particular motivation comes with both positive and negative impacts. In the clinical literature on this topic, it is acknowledged that trauma can negatively impact practitioners when working with traumatised clients. However, that same literature goes on to affirm the following:

2 Mary Dale Salston and Charles R Figley, 'Secondary traumatic stress effects of working with survivors of criminal victimization', *Journal of Traumatic Stress*, Vol 16, No 2, April 2003, pp167–174 (C 2003) at pp172–173.

At the same time, they may show particular strengths in working with survivors. A wounded healer may attain a deeper understanding of the dynamics of a specific trauma as a direct result of having endured a comparable traumatic experience.[3]

In-depth studies on this issue have explored various tensions that can arise for practitioners who bring their own trauma experiences to their work, for example tensions between:

– showing empathy and maintaining professional distance;
– establishing and maintaining a professional role, whilst balancing client expectations and needs, and a personal desire to connect;
– the politicisation of lawyering when you yourself are a trauma survivor versus the need to focus on client interests and wellbeing.[4]

While further in-depth study of this intersection falls outside the scope of this book, it is important to note that past trauma can both intensify the experience of client trauma *and* equip practitioners empathically.

> 'So vicarious trauma, it does tie into some of the reasons why I entered this field of work ... sometimes it is a good thing because I feel I can empathise with some of the clients I have. However, it does make me reflect on personal experiences that I have had and that can be a re-traumatising situation for me.
>
> It is also very daunting, some of the instructions I receive and trying to be professional at the same time as trying to be personable – that mix is hard.
>
> Some of the stories you hear do haunt you for time to come, just because they are so awful.'
>
> *Solicitor*

It can also – particularly with state-sanctioned or systemic trauma – be exhausting to observe the continued trauma meted out against the group to which a practitioner also belongs. For example, a practi-

3 Yael Fischman, PhD, 'Secondary trauma in the legal professions, a clinical perspective', *TORTURE*, Volume 18, Number 2, 2008 p108: https://irct.org/assets/uploads/1018-8185_2008-2_107-115.pdf.
4 Kelly Jo Popkin, 'Survivors representing survivors: shared experience and identity in direct service lawyering', 5 LMU Law Review 1 (2017).

tioner who is a survivor of a domestically abusive relationship witnessing the escalation of cases of domestic abuse during the 2020 COVID-19 pandemic lockdowns;[5] or a practitioner who is a former refugee watching the grotesque news coverage of asylum-seekers and migrants arriving in rubber dinghies across the Channel during the summer of 2020;[6] or practitioners who are Black or people of colour experiencing repeated racist micro-aggressions within their workplaces.

It can feel like nothing improves, that your work in service of vulnerable groups is a drop in the ocean, or that our justice system will continue to marginalise and abuse the most vulnerable, which, for practitioners who have experienced trauma themselves, can be re-traumatising.

The force and breadth of the media coverage of human-inflicted trauma and atrocity can also be inescapable.

> 'It is so hard to have a good work life balance when you work in civil liberties / human rights areas. You almost feel like you have to be fighting every battle that is out there. You are trying to fight the battle with work, then you go on Twitter and there are 10 more things to be upset and enraged about and so you are trying to deal with all of those things too. It is never ending, the number of issues you can engage with and try to contribute to. It kind of feels like it is never ending, which is a very depressing way of dealing with things.'
>
> *Paralegal*

For many, this is compounded by the hostile environment advocated by the current government against 'activist lawyers' and legal redress generally,[7] including the explicit 'hostile environment policy' adopted by the Home Office under the leadership of then Home Secretary,

5 'Survivors say domestic abuse is escalating under lockdown', Woman's Aid, 28 April 2020: www.womensaid.org.uk/survivors-say-domestic-abuse-is-escalating-under-lockdown/.

6 J Waterson, 'BBC and Sky accused of 'voyeurism' in coverage of migrant boats', *The Guardian*, 11 August 2020: www.theguardian.com/uk-news/2020/aug/11/bbc-and-sky-accused-of-dehumanising-people-trying-to-cross-channel.

7 J Hyde, 'Home Office accuses 'activist lawyers' of abusing immigration rules', *Law Society Gazette*, 27 August 2020: www.lawgazette.co.uk/news/home-office-accuses-activist-lawyers-of-abusing-immigration-rules/5105437.article.

Theresa May – a policy which (at the time of writing) is under investigation by the Equality and Human Rights Commission (EHRC) for breach of equality law.[8]

This narrowing of legal scope and opportunity to achieve justice for vulnerable groups, coupled with government-endorsed media backlash against those groups, can be deeply demoralising.

> 'The way I deal with [the trauma] is to be practical. For me the tonic has been that I am not there as a silent observer, but that I am actually doing something. I think that what I find most distressing is the cases where you can't achieve anything for your clients. I would find it very difficult to do immigration cases these days because it's got to a stage where you cannot achieve a just outcome because the law is so set against your clients. I think that is the most stressful thing. I can cope with the trauma I observe because I am trying to do something about it and trying to make things better.'
>
> *Solicitor*

Conversely, the horror attendant to this work can be a huge source of motivation:

> '. . . the moment the work doesn't upset me anymore, the moment that I don't feel anything, will be the moment I give up this type of practice. The distress of my clients motivates me to try to make it better.'
>
> *Solicitor*

8 A Gentleman, 'Equalities watchdog to investigate hostile environment policy', *The Guardian*, 12 June 2020: www.theguardian.com/uk-news/2020/jun/12/equalities-watchdog-to-investigate-hostile-environment-policy.

It is for many, the very reason they entered the profession:

> '[For me, this work is about] protecting my lay clients, developing a narrative and articulating a narrative for their circumstances. It's trying to deconstruct their behaviours so they're portrayed as less culpable. In some ways I am a champion or a support for my clients.
>
> *Barrister*

What is important to recognise is that whatever we bring to our work, we are all operating in systems that can be – and often are – entirely hostile to the ends we are trying to achieve for our clients. That takes its toll. Connecting back to the reasons you do this work is a crucial and protective pushback.

Why do we begin here?

In examining the contexts in which we work, we start here, at the beginning, at the motivations stage, because it is often our personal contexts that bring us to this work.

What emerges from a consideration of the structural pressures placed upon practising lawyers in this area, is that these pressures can actively prevent lawyers from achieving just outcomes for clients. This has the effect of distancing practitioners from both their motivation to do this work and the protection and resilience that such motivation should provide.

The impact of this is manifold, from: increasing the chance of employee burnout as it becomes impossible for individuals to create – or have available to them – the resources to meet demand; to destabilising practitioners' sense of purpose, drive or ability to do their work.[9]

Ultimately it can cause or contribute to burnout:

Burnout can be caused by conflict between individual values and organizational goals and demands, an overload of responsibilities, a sense of having no control over the quality of services provided, awareness of little emotional or financial reward, a sense of a loss of community within the work setting, and the existence of inequity or lack of respect at the workplace (Maslach & Leiter, 1997). Often times, the individuals who experience burnout are highly idealistic about the

9 Rønning, Blumberg and Dammeyer, 2020.

way in which they can help others (Pines & Aronson, 1988). Burnout also can be related to consistent exposure to traumatic material (Aguilera, 1995).[10]

We have – in brief – considered each of the critical structural pressures that come to bear on lawyers working with vulnerable populations, as listed above.

We note that in the inter-country research conducted by Rønning, Blumberg and Dammeyer in their 2020 study, 'Vicarious traumatisation in lawyers working with traumatised asylum seekers: a pilot study', the following theme emerged:

> In addition, over the last decade, there have been steady cuts to legal aid, social care and health service funding and the closure of voluntary sector organisations. Cumulatively, these factors place an additional burden on asylum lawyers, who must advocate for their vulnerable and traumatised clients with significantly reduced resources (N. Acharya, personal communication, May 15, 2017), potentially resulting in an increased risk of VT to legal professionals working with this client group.

We agree.

We posit that these issues are not confined to immigration and asylum law, but are sector-wide, and that further longitudinal study of the structural pressures of working in this field and traumatic workloads is required.

Education, training and remuneration

It is an open secret that legal education and training is exceptionally expensive. The effects of this on social mobility are clearly set out in the reports on this topic by YLAL, to name one resource.

YLAL has – since its inception – written and campaigned extensively in support of social mobility, advocating that our justice system must be representative of the clients it serves and that true social mobility within the legal profession is yet to be realised.

---

10 Mary Dale Salston and Charles R Figley, 'Secondary traumatic stress effects of working with survivors of criminal victimization', *Journal of Traumatic Stress*, Vol 16, No 2, April 2003, pp67–174 (C° 2003) at p168.

In its most recent report, 'Young Legal Aid Lawyers: Social mobility in a time of austerity'[11] published in 2018, YLAL highlighted three key issues:

1) '*Debt combined with low salaries is a barrier to the profession.*' '72 per cent of respondents have or will have debt over £15,000 as a result of their education and 26.5 per cent will have over £35,000.' This is an increase of 7 per cent and 11.5 per cent respectively, since their last report in 2013. 53 per cent of respondents earn less than £25,000 per year with 30 per cent earning below £20,000. Respondents listed low pay as the biggest challenge facing young lawyers in the legal aid sector.

2) '*Unpaid work experience is a barrier to the profession.*' '13.5 per cent of respondents cited unpaid work experience as having been a barrier to entry to the profession.'

3) '*Stress, lack of support and juggling legal aid work with other responsibilities are affecting retention in the profession.* Stress was the second most common problem faced by our respondents; 21 per cent said this was the biggest challenge they experienced.'[12]

The identification of these issues followed a membership-wide survey in which many respondents cited the pernicious effects of the legal aid funding cuts introduced by the Legal Aid, Sentencing and Punishment of Offenders Act 2012 (LASPO). Respondents described LASPO as having pushed them out of the profession, as firms and individuals struggled to manage debt levels, low pay and low morale. The findings of this report built on the previous YLAL social mobility report published in 2013, a time when LASPO was just bedding in.

What emerges from the YLAL reports and other supporting studies is a high-debt, low-pay scenario for many new entrants to the profession. This is toxic in effect, particularly where workloads are traumatic.

---

11 *Young Legal Aid Lawyers: Social mobility in a time of austerity*, March 2018: www.younglegalaidlawyers.org/sites/default/files/Soc%20Mob%20Report%20-%20edited.pdf.

12 At: www.younglegalaidlawyers.org/socialmobilityreport2018.

'The other side of stress, which comes with the job, is just the practical fact that it is so low paid. There is the stress that is in the work – you know that is inherently in the work – stress, vulnerable clients etc. But such low pay to do such long hours and such emotionally draining work?'

Paralegal

Some practitioners reading this text may consider that decisions about high course fees and low wages are not in their gift to change. However, there is anecdotal and growing concern that firms are becoming apathetic or – at worst – callous in their approach to junior practitioners who find themselves vulnerable to these toxic pressures.

'At the start of lockdown my firm was monitoring time recording daily. It was so stressful. Sometimes you just may not have that work. It's never allowing for a off day.

My friends find it mad that I work so many hours with no overtime, no bonus, no monetary benefit.

. . . I feel like a lot of firms know that there is such a surplus of people aspiring to work in social justice and that they are willing to exploit our desire to work in this area. We all want to do this work, that's why we stick it out – firms know that and they are complicit. I know there have been huge cuts [to legal aid], but some firms do manage to make it worthwhile, for their benefit.'

Paralegal

There are also legitimate concerns about the transparency of remuneration for legal professionals. Such was the concern about this opacity on new entrants to the profession that YLAL introduced a new policy in 2016 of only advertising jobs on its much frequented jobs page where the salary was advertised.[13] It is also an issue that reportedly causes resentment and division within firms:

13 See: www.younglegalaidlawyers.org/legal_aid_work.

'A huge source of stress and anger and discord between staff: [is] lack of pay transparency across the firm.

I earn a substantial amount more [than others in] the team, I don't earn much, but I earn more than the other paralegals who are paid pretty much nothing.

I think there should be a lot more transparency about what people are paid. We should be paid the living wage, at the very least. Again, because we are expendable, they don't really care. I am lucky in terms of [the partner] who I work with, they will fight for something if it's unfair, but only for their own paralegal, which makes inequalities.

Be honest about what you're paying people.'

Paralegal

We are not suggesting that firms bear sole responsibility for the issues attendant to legal education, training and remuneration – but it is important to acknowledge the importance of taking all steps within firms' control to deal with these issues, for example: pay transparency, and proper remuneration, wherever possible. There is a real concern that a failure to do so is likely to increase the exclusion from the profession of applicants for lower socio-economic or working class background, not least because their longevity in the profession may be compromised by being unable to pay for necessary additional support, such as talking therapy.

At the very least it must be recognised that this is an additional structural pressure on many new entrants to the profession, one that should be factored into work-based policies, risk assessments and the management of traumatic caseloads.

Another critical issue in the current legal education and training framework is notable in its absence: *education and training on trauma-informed working*. This absence was identified again and again by young entrants to the profession who we interviewed for this book. The demand and the need for training in this area could not be clearer.

'My anxiety stemmed from not being trained. You are expected to know how to do everything in your role, which is ok if you have people to support you. But at the time I did not have that support for my role.'

Former paralegal

'The main [thing that would allow me to function safely in my role] is definitely more training. Even at the beginning, having more training in the most basic sense: these are the things you might have to deal with, the situations you might be in – just kind of a heads up. You know it's not going to be sunshine and rainbows, but in the first few weeks of my job I would be on my own with clients sharing horrible things, even just personal things from their lives that they wanted to offload. There is no training on how to speak to clients – and it is different when it's a client; they are not just a normal person. The things you say matter. There is so much scope for better training on what to say when someone is saying something awful. Some sort of guide on when / how you should act.'

Paralegal

'I think obviously training would be an easy one. All aspects of client care should be so much more of a focus. It should not be something you learn on the job – I feel so strongly about this – everyone has different social skills.'

Paralegal

'I think it would be really good if there were mandatory training courses on vicarious trauma before caseworkers even pick up a case which involves any level of vulnerability.'

Solicitor

This applies to everyone: from students who work in legal clinics as part of their clinical practice training; to trainee solicitors; to pupil barristers; to caseworkers and paralegals starting out; and to legal executives.

We would argue that while this book focusses on lawyers, the issues herein – and certainly the need for training – extends to clerking and support staff in the organisations we work.

'The job sometimes does take its toll. Dealing with your barristers and their mental health and their stress, trying to care for them but not having the skills to do it. You worry about that. You worry about work coming in, too much work, not enough work, people getting upset about the work they get – it's on you. Generally mental health is always there … I think [for me] there have been dips and troughs with it; it's a stressful job all round. Chambers and clerking does not really know how to deal with it. It's not an issue clerks will be informed about, not something that is really mentioned.'

Clerk

'I interviewed for a job in an abuse team at a big firm. I asked them what the firm does to try and help people process this stuff and they said that one of the PAs was a really good listener if you need to talk to someone. So a) they have no proper provision and b) they are encouraging you to dump this all on support staff.'

Solicitor

Legal aid funding

There are numerous legal aid funding issues that place continued and acute pressure on the nature and conduct of legal casework. These are aptly summarised in Rønning, Blumberg and Dammeyer (2020):[14]

> In this study, participants routinely discussed high caseloads, legal aid cuts, and discussions about the financial viability of their firms. These became recurring themes of discussion. For example, one participant described the asylum legal sector as 'overwhelmed', whereas another participant described how practitioners needed to have larger caseloads to make firms financially viable because of the 'extreme restrictions on legal aid'. Another participant stated 'we just didn't have the capacity to take all those people … I think our caseload was just not manageable, was unsustainable'. A number of participants spoke directly about cuts to legal aid affecting their work.

14 Rønning L, Blumberg J, Dammeyer J (2020). 'Vicarious traumatisation in lawyers working with traumatised asylum seekers: a pilot study', *Psychiatry, Psychology and Law*.

These cuts clearly had an impact on practitioners as they were required to take on additional cases or were working in increasingly financially precarious environments. These structural issues were discussed by many of the participants in the study and appeared as important to their ability to cope with the emotional demands of their work than other issues. This gave the impression that whilst there were heavy emotional demands of working with traumatised people or hearing traumatic narratives, there were wider issues within the asylum law sector which were directly impacting on individuals, causing stress.

The history and development of legal aid policy, the narrowing of the scope of funding, and the increased requirement for firms to specialise in order to retain their legal aid contracts, is explored with depth and rigour by Hynes and Robins in their 2009 text, *The justice gap: whatever happened to legal aid?*[15] and further by Hynes in his 2012 text, *Austerity justice.*[16]

What is striking from the Hynes and Robins texts – for our purposes – is that:

- Changes to legal aid contracting have required firms to specialise to maintain their practices. The impact of this is clear across the sector and is adeptly set out by one practitioner interviewed for this book:

'When I was a trainee in private practice you could see the glimmer of decades gone by when people could almost be general practitioners of the law: you could do a variety of work and one could envisage using legal skills across a variety of specialisms, some of which would be distressing, but some of which wouldn't. However, the reality of the franchising that came in in the 1990s and the requirements from Legal Aid Agency to really specialise to maintain your contract has removed for many the possibility of spreading your work between practice areas that range from less stressful to traumatizing areas of work. It is hardly possible to do that anymore.'

Solicitor

---

15 Hynes and Robins, 2009. *The Justice Gap: Whatever happened to legal aid?* Legal Action Group, London.
16 Hynes, 2012. *Austerity Justice.* Legal Action Group, London.

- LASPO has reduced the scope of funding so that only the most traumatic areas of law continue to be funded.
- Legal advice and service 'deserts' have emerged following firm, law centre and court closures.
- Fixed fees have remained static in many areas of law for in excess of 10 years.

The impact of this for firms who operate with very tight margins, cannot be overstated. It is perhaps unsurprising, as Rønning, Blumberg and Dammeyer (2020) observe, that neglecting trauma training and supervision is a natural corollary of the need of firms to cost-save in order to stay afloat. Although further research and analysis would be needed to prove this, it may well be that such investment would have an overall net benefit: people who are working with vicarious trauma or burnout may be less efficient fee earners. For example, they are slower at billing a case because they are avoiding re-visiting the traumatic facts or their memory is impacted to the extent that routine tasks take longer. Whilst our arguments for broad systemic change in the legal profession are not driven by a motivation to improve fee income, such a benefit may allow for broader adoption of much-needed strategies and investment.

It can readily be observed that in this context, practitioners are being asked to do more with less; to take on extra traumatic cases to keep firms viable; and to work within fee structures that fossilised many years ago. There is also the added pressure that practitioners may feel that they should take on cases because clients have nowhere else to go, which has obvious practical and emotional repercussions.

> 'I am still at that stage, 15 years into my career, where I am just taking on cases I would ideally not take on because no one else is there to refer them to, but I do not want to leave a desperate person without the legal support they need. So the depletion of the sector and the number of providers is a huge problem.'
>
> *Solicitor*

Proper funding, re-scoping of legal aid provision and adequate remuneration are absolute necessities. However, this is also extremely unlikely to occur. Years of austerity have eroded the fifth and most unloved pillar of the welfare state – legal aid – and there is little optimism that that will change.

What is also striking is the impact that increased bureaucracy within the current underfunded system has on organisational and trauma management. This was a frequent source of discontent and disconnect on the part of junior practitioners interviewed for this book, and a great source of stress for managers tasked with ensuring that all legal aid contractual requirements were met, to the letter.

CW: self-harm

'I think the bureaucracy of the legal aid requirements is a massive exacerbating factor and that the two things [the bureaucracy and the stress / burnout / vicarious trauma issues] are really linked.

When people are busting a gut to really try and make a substantive difference and they feel like they are doing something really important, to switch your mind to make sure the form is all filled in, or getting that bank statement to prove that a penniless client really doesn't have a bean to their name, that level of bureaucracy and distrust causes a real stress.

It also means that as a manager you've got to be really hot on that stuff and it reverberates down. The natural reaction of someone who is working really hard with incredibly traumatic things to, "you haven't filled in this form properly", is, "well hang on, I have just read 100 pages of incredibly distressing material, I have spent hours on phone with a mother who was crying, I have been with a client with self-harm scars so bad that I hardly knew where to look and you're moaning about a form?!".'

Solicitor

It may be said that this particular disconnect or pressure invites – and in fact requires – communication between different levels of practitioner in a firm: about their respective roles and remit, and about the different pressures that they are each under in that role. However, we wish to make clear that this is first and foremost another stark example of the systems in which practitioners must work: systems that divide and rule, and wear practitioners down.

Leaving the profession

It should be a matter of significant concern across the profession that lawyers *are* leaving the profession because of the lack of support and acknowledgement of these issues. This is a tragedy for those who entered the profession with the motivation and drive to succeed and to effect real change; and, for the clients who no longer have access to that talent.

First, there is the concern about losing talented lawyers – often at the junior end of the profession – for preventable reasons. There are financial and morale costs of high turnover. Second, we owe our colleagues and comrades a healthy and fair workplace.

'I felt quite resentful by the end which isn't a nice way to be living. It feels like such a shame. There were so many aspects of the work I loved. I don't have clients anymore and I really miss the clients. I don't feel fulfilled in the same way, but I find it hard to believe there is any happy medium. I don't know where I would go to do something sustainable working on the same types of issues for the same group of clients.

I did end up leaving this sector of the profession because of the emotional toll of working with traumatised clients. On top of that there is the stress imposed on you by a firm that is making money out of you, without any recognition of what it means to be working with this group of people.'

Solicitor

Reflecting on 2020

It is an inescapable fact of writing in 2020 that we are living in a global pandemic. The true impact of COVID-19 on our work; on the viability of firms, law centres and collateral organisations that work with vulnerable populations; and, on us as people and lawyers, is unknown.

The immediate issue that has affected many – if not all – practitioners has been the requirement to work from home during much or all of the lockdown periods, the first of which commenced on 23 March 2020. This has profoundly changed the patterns and pressures of our working day even before any consideration is given to the additional caring responsibilities, sickness or worry that living through a pandemic has created for so many, particularly Black and minority ethnic (BAME) people (as described in the UK press), who have been disproportionately affected by COVID-19.[17]

The British Psychological Society has highlighted its concern about working with distressing material in a home environment. In response to this concern, it has created and issued a guidance document for employers and employees how to manage these issues.[18] These issues are real, and they require specific and separate management by firms and organisations, many of which are in disarray and growing difficulties as the pandemic continues.

There is significant anecdotal concern about how to maintain trauma-informed working structures when people are working from home.

> 'We have rearranged the desks so that more junior members of staff are sitting in a central island, sitting next to each other. That opened up dialogues and allowed people to hear each other if they were having to deal with something distressing. It opened up conversation and support without having to go to someone to say that ... These have been the most important things. Trying to replicate or match that during COVID-19 has been very difficult.'
>
> *Solicitor*

In these unprecedented times, we also experienced the extraordinary rise of the Black Lives Matter movement. This followed the circulation of video footage of an unarmed Black man, George Floyd, being killed by police officers on the streets of Minneapolis, US, on 25 May 2020. The response was overwhelming, and for many it came much

---

17 Niamh McIntyre, Aamna Mohdin and Tobi Thomas, 'BAME workers disproportionately hit by UK Covid-19 downturn, data shows', *The Guardian*, 4 August 2020: www.theguardian.com/society/2020/aug/04/bame-workers-disproportionately-hit-uk-economic-downturn-data-shows-coronavirus.

18 'Taking trauma related work home – advice for reducing the likelihood of secondary trauma', British Psychological Society, 10 June 2020: www.bps.org.uk/coronavirus-resources/professional/taking-trauma-home.

too late, there having been so many unlawful killings of Black people in the US and the UK prior to George Floyd and so many more since.

We make clear that we write this book as two white cis women. With that comes significant privilege, and no personal insight or experience of structural or interpersonal racism. We do know that racism is as a force against our clients, our colleagues and our friends. We note that many Black people and people of colour have described the disappointment, anger and exhaustion of this issue only coming to public consciousness when a video of a Black man dying in the street was widely circulated on social media.[19]

As anti-oppression campaigner, trainer and barrister, Raggi Kotak,[20] describes, racism – overt and covert – is a present part of our courts and the state systems in which we operate. Decisive and meaningful action is required now. Unless we are anti-racist in our work practice, we cannot claim to be 'trauma-informed' or 'trauma-sensitive'.

How and where this intersects with our traumatic caseloads is a complex issue. What is clear is that it presents yet another factor that has a particular bearing on vulnerable and marginal populations, Black people and people of colour, and that it affects many clients and practitioners alike.

19 'Comment: being non-racist is not enough', *Freemovement*, 26 August 2020: www.freemovement.org.uk/comment-being-non-racist-is-not-enough-we-must-be-active-anti-racists/.

20 Ibid 19. Bar Standards Board, press release, 'BSB Race Equality Taskforce launches series of case studies to promote racial diversity and inclusion at the Bar', 29 July 2020: www.barstandardsboard.org.uk/resources/ press-releases/ bsb-raceequality-taskforce-launches-series-of-case-studies-to-promote-racial-diversityand-inclusion-at-the-bar.html.

PART II

Action

CHAPTER 8

Raising awareness and creating supportive cultures

> "I was hoping in my childish immature wisdom that I would somehow kick the can down the road, but it hits you in a way you don't expect. You'll no longer be functioning, no longer responding to emails, no longer doing the really really simple tasks on a case: the attendance notes and so on."
>
> *Barrister*

We do not intend to tell you what you should do or how you should act on these issues. Each person and each organisation is different, both in terms of needs, culture and resources.

However, the first and critical step is *awareness*. This may sound trite, but it is not. Stress, burnout and vicarious trauma are real issues. People in your workplace are – to varying degrees – experiencing these phenomena right now. The effect can and does impede the basic functioning of practitioners. Coming to terms with that fact is crucial for effective practice management, client care and practitioner safety.

> 'I have had some moments where I do think it [my workload] is unachievable; those are the almost-at-breaking-point burnout moments. It is often when I have got loads of competing deadlines – you do kind of feel like you are drowning.'
>
> *Solicitor*

Trauma-informed approaches to working

A useful framework for organisations working with trauma is the 'trauma-informed approach'.[1]

In summary, trauma-informed organisations will:

- realise the prevalence of trauma;
- recognise the impact of trauma;

---

1 Substance Abuse and Mental Health Services Administration, *SAMHSA's Concept of trauma and guidance for a trauma-informed approach*, HHS Publication No (SMA) 14-4884. Rockville, MD: Substance Abuse and Mental Health Services Administration, 2014; https://store.samhsa.gov/product/SAMHSA-s-Concept-of-Trauma-and-Guidance-for-a-Trauma-Informed-Approach/SMA14-4884.

- respond across the system;
- resist re-traumatisation (both client and practitioner).

What does this mean for legal practice?

Realise prevalence

Trauma-informed approaches are based on an understanding of the prevalence of trauma. The statistics show a rate of five per cent of UK adults experiencing post-traumatic stress disorder (PTSD) symptoms to a clinical level (and one might therefore assume another significant section experiencing significant but subclinical symptomatology affecting their day-to-day life). More broadly, we can estimate that around one-third of adults have experienced a traumatic event (as defined by the DSM[2] criteria see p15), within the general population.

It is reasonable to assume a similar rate within entrants to the profession and, generally, much higher in our clients. In some areas of practice it may be close to 100 per cent of clients having recently experienced a traumatic event with the protential to cause a post-traumatic stress response). In combination, and on the research currently available, it is not only reasonable but necessary to acknowledge the widespread effect of traumatic events on those we work alongside, even if we personally have not had such experiences.

Recognise impact

We are in the early stages of understanding the full impact of trauma in the legal profession, but the evidence to date is sufficiently alarming.

Recognising the impact of trauma means having spaces where we feel able to have honest discussions about it and taking vicarious trauma into account in all aspects of our working. For example, when a lawyer is not 'performing' (eg not meeting time recording targets; missing deadlines on cases; being absent from responsibilities in chambers) is the first point of call to implement disciplinary measures; or does the organisation have systems in place to assess any link between caseload, trauma and performance?

This recognition must extend across the organisation, from clients to fee earners to support staff.

---

2 *Diagnostic and statistical manual of mental disorders*, 5th edn, American Psychiatric Association, 2013.

We do not need to attempt to diagnose clients, rather to practise in a way that recognises the potential impact on our clients so that we can best support them. For a client, avoidance might manifest in being late to or missing appointments, or avoiding answering questions (although of course there may be a number of other reasons for this!). A client might express the impact of trauma in ways that are unfamiliar to us – for example, slower movement, shaking or even laughter.

While experienced practitioners may quickly recognise features of trauma, this is not routinely included in training for entrants to the profession or for support staff.

Respond across the system

As we set out above and below, neither trauma nor resilience are individual phenomena, but rather collective. If we understand trauma as a systemic issue, the wider limbs of the justice system would also respond (can we imagine a trauma-informed Legal Aid Agency?). We set out below suggestions of how we might respond on a team, organisational and profession-wide level.

'We got a report through on [an] inquiry and it had very horrible and graphic pictures in it. I was asked to review it . . . it was not clear that there would be all these images in the report.

I could imagine in my head what [the images] would look like, but I was reviewing the report, I was relatively new in the job – I'd been there a couple of months – and it was all very awful.

I did this summary of [the report], sent it to my boss and he said, "maybe you shouldn't have looked at that". Then he said, "oh sorry, I hope you're OK, you should have known about that before". But it was only in retrospect he thought of that.

If I had been warned I could have thought about how appropriate it was for me to read the report or whether I wanted to. It wasn't intentional, but it happened and I had zero preparation about what I was about to see. I thought, "am I supposed to not be affected by this and that's why he's [my boss has] given me this task, so I shouldn't make it a big deal?'

Paralegal

Resist re-traumatisation

This approach also acknowledges the risk of re-traumatisation by the system of those within it. For example, when our approach to taking a client or witness's evidence is unnecessarily re-traumatising for them, it will negatively affect us too. Conversely, our own active hyper-arousal / traumatised state may be contagious (co-regulation). See 'The Client' section below at page 122.

Challenges of change

Sweeney et al[3] set out several challenges to implementing and developing trauma-informed practice in mental healthcare in the UK, which readily apply to the challenges facing the legal profession:

- resistance from those who do not believe in the effect of trauma;
- acknowledging the full impact within the profession also involves facing both the full 'horror' and the extent of cultural change necessary;
- change is resource-intensive;
- resistance from those who benefit from the status quo;
- superficial acknowledgement of principles of trauma-informed working / impact of vicarious trauma, without systemic change and ongoing support.

3 A Sweeney, S Clement, B Filson and A Kennedy, 'Trauma-informed mental healthcare in the UK: what is it and how can we further its development?', Mental Health Review Journal, (2016) Vol 21 No 3, pp174–192; https://doi.org/10.1108/MHRJ-01-2015-0006.

'At one firm I worked at, we had a half day training . . . which was helpful, but the actual practices of that firm were so horrendous, there is no point in sending someone on a training when the workplace is so stressful. It felt like it was for show.

At another firm they were starting to think a bit more about these issues. They were listening to us but they wanted a one-off solution rather than to do what is necessary which is to employ somebody to be there to give people time [for supervision]. I know it happens in other sectors, so why can't it happen in the legal profession?

Employers say they want to work on it but they want a cheap, easy, outward solution instead of a real commitment to looking after staff.'

Solicitor

Taking stock of these experiences is undoubtedly difficult. For our own part, we found conducting interviews in preparation for this book profoundly affecting, humbling and often triggering of our own work experiences, past and present.

We recognise that change is going to be difficult. But we also recognise that widespread change is needed across the profession. This is about a cultural, organisational, and system awakening to the presence and urgency of these issues.

When entering into that difficult space of working to effect change, we stress that this is first and foremost a *collective issue*. Although it requires individual action, meaningful change cannot be achieved by individual practitioners on their own, not least because there is a unique power to peer support and collective action.

In the first instance, there are simple things that can help raise awareness and understanding of these issues, for example:

- mindfulness-based practices;
- time for self-reflection;
- self-care;
- reflective practice;
- peer support;
- informal/formal support;
- supervision;
- trauma-informed supervision;
- individual therapy.

All of the above help move towards trauma-informed practice. We will unpack some of these techniques in this 'action' section of the book.

Creating cultures where there is regular time and space to reflect

How can we create such cultures?

- **Ensuring that all members of these professions have the language to be able to discuss these issues.** Reading this book, having conversations about these issues, exploring terms, ideas, concepts and methods of communication, are all very important steps.
- **Educating ourselves, even if currently we do not consider ourselves to be 'personally' affected, knowing that it does certainly affect our colleagues and clients.** This is about individual and collective wellbeing; preparing for the now and the future.

> 'I think ultimately the thing that has made the real difference to me is knowing that nobody in my team is alone with the particular facts of the case or a set of photographs, that everything is shared. That opens up a dialogue for shared experience and reactions to something.'
>
> *Solicitor*

- **Creating permission and appropriate outlets to discuss these issues.**

'There is still a lot of stigma in law . . . it is still clear that we are expected to just "get on". If the tasks needs doing, you are expected to do it, to get on with it. There are not many facilities or systems set up if you are struggling. They [firms, managers, supervisors] point you towards LawCare on day one, give you a little leaflet and ask you in supervisions superficially how are you, but beyond that there are no mental health advocates, even things like yoga sessions, or lunches across the firm. No initiatives that would encourage open discussions.'

Paralegal

'By support I mean not just support for my workload, but personally, so if I can say to someone, I am having a difficult day or something is making me nervous or I am a bit stressed out about something. I feel that you also need to be comfortable enough telling someone and to know that you have that person's support and that they will listen to you. Saying that out loud makes me realise it's ridiculous we don't have that set up, because the work we do is so important, and having that set up in place would make such a difference.'

Pupil barrister

- **Senior members of the profession modelling good practice.** There is also a need for senior members of the profession to acknowledge the power that they hold within organisations, as against the powerlessness and lack of control that junior practitioners have or feel about the nature and content of their caseload and how that is managed.

'I would also say I think generally there needs to be a shift in attitude in workplaces in terms of whether or not someone can cope with what they are given, so the best way to explain that: if you have inherited a large caseload, it is not your choice to have so many cases, so it is being aware of that when requesting / asking that further cases be added on top of that. Be more respectful and mindful of people's capacity.'

Solicitor

- **Ensuring that all learning and reflection is facilitated in a way that explicitly and implicitly acknowledges and takes account of the intersectionality of trauma.** This includes an awareness that the ability of an individual to engage in personal healing is also enabled or inhibited because of personal and societal factors. Ultimately a trauma-informed workplace can be of benefit for all.

'Having the open dialogue – and also thinking about things that might be triggering the personal experience of practitioners or where someone might have or particularly disability, making sure that person does not <u>have</u> to deal with a particular case that deals with that issue [if they don't wish to do so], is very important.'

Solicitor

- **Never presuming that we can know the experience of a colleague, or what would be a suitable response for them** – for example, presuming that someone with personal experience of a type of discrimination either should or should not undertake work in that area or that all relevant experiences will be apparent or disclosable to employers.
- **Acknowledging that we do not all have to agree, or list the same symptoms, or be able to put a particular label to our experience (or reject a particular label) in order to collectively support each other.** The fact that there is no one answer, no easy solution, can create additional unease – but there is often the potential for great creativity and connection when space is held for all the differences.
- **Creating trauma-informed client care, ethics and personnel policies.** Trauma-informed practice can, and should, be embedded at all levels of an organisation. Clear policies should be in place for any employee dealing with traumatic material. Training should be provided at the point of induction and when any employee takes on management or supervisory responsibilities.
- **Ensuring that there is space for the appreciation and cultivation of the positive aspects of the work.** Celebrate the wins! However big or small. Positive feedback is immensely important to practitioner wellbeing and has important implications in developing the 'positive' effects of vicarious trauma: compassion satisfaction.

- **The opposite is also true – appreciating the negative power of derision of fellow practitioners is extremely important.** It is hypocritical in the extreme for human rights firms and lawyers to enable and promote workplace bullying, but it happens, frequently. The impact of this cannot be overstated.

'For me – wanting to become a barrister – I put a lot of pressure on myself to get there. I think if you add to that pressure by having someone you work with who tells you you're not good enough – or any sort of negative comments – it may add to stress or anxiety, or maybe something worse than that. Luckily it wasn't worse than that for me. I think some senior members of the profession need to take this into account when working with junior members.'

Pupil barrister

'There are also experiences that I look back on and realise were quite toxic working environments, but at the time I was fresh, enthusiastic and motivated so felt fine . . . If a junior lawyer was in that position now I'd give them very strong advice about whether that would be healthy for them.'

Casework consultant

- **Normalising a range of responses** – in a profession which is in many ways diverse, it still sits within a white supremacist, patriarchal structure that rewards particular responses to distress (ignoring it, repressing it and – most dangerously – displacing it in bullying behaviour).

'Law is still such an old-fashioned profession. It is still dominated by white middleclass men. With a new generation of lawyers there can be a shift, but it won't happen unless start talking about this and start changing the culture. No more stiff upper lip.'

Paralegal

- **Separating our sense of self-worth from the case we are working on.** Recognising that your worth as a person or as a lawyer is not tied to the outcome of the case, that there is worth in your having been an advocate for the client, having believed them and having their case presented well. We accept that this can be difficult – more so in some types of cases – but is a critical distinction to draw and boundary to maintain.

'[Something] I find incredibly stressful is when – particularly in a care [public law children] case – you're the only one fighting in one direction and everyone else in room is fighting in the other direction. It is incredibly stressful, it's incredibly lonely. . . It is hard not to feel that it's personal, even though your rational mind knows it's about your case, it's about the evidence in the case; the rational mind knows it's about your client's position in that case. But I think you feel – I really feel – for my client in those situations. Almost when the evidence is more over-whelming, you have to fight harder for them to get a fair trial. Sometimes I feel like the other professionals are putting you in your client's bracket: the judge is looking at you with utter contempt or will stop you in your cross examination even though you're putting the case you're instructed to put. I think that adds to your sense of stress.'

Barrister

Reflective practice

The basis of much of what follows is in essence a call to develop a more *reflective practice* as the norm in the legal profession. We cannot begin to take better care of ourselves and each other if we do not regularly and as a matter of habit enable space for reflection on how we are, how our work as a legal practitioner is developing, and how the work may be impacting us.

As we have set out above, if the effects are much more than personal, then this reflection must also extend beyond the individual. Reflective practice can happen in a brief moment in the day, or be the focus of substantial professional development training (eg a day-long training).

What is set out below refers to the issues that we have considered in this book – however, it may be more practical or even beneficial to incorporate reflection on the emotional impact of the work with reflection on the strengths and limitations of our legal practice more broadly. The continuing professional development (CPD) model for the legal profession in England and Wales requires an element of reflective learning.

There are various models of reflective practice and learning (eg Gibbs' reflective cycle; Kolb's learning cycle). We propose a model below that could be used or adapted for legal practice.

Space for reflection

1) Creating the right conditions for reflection

This will depend on the particular format of the space.

- A brief 'grounding practice' like the one we opened the book with can be done anywhere – no one needs to know you are doing it.
- Informal debrief with a supervisor following a difficult incident on a case.
- A regular space for colleagues to discuss issues will have different needs for conditions.
- Private, confidential sessions with a qualified mental health practitioner.

2) Inquiring

- How did I feel?
- What thoughts came up?
- What emotions were present?
- What sensations could I feel in my body?

3) Sharing

- An optional level, not always appropriate for every type of reflection.
- A personal reflection may be supported by journaling or expressing in another way (creative activity, singing/dancing/art, physical expression/exercise, yoga, etc),

(See peer support, debriefing and supervision sections.)

4) Integration

Unfortunately there are no quick fixes. Developing new practices that genuinely support individuals, teams and organisations take time and effort.

Questions we might consider are:

- Does our formal peer support include a feedback loop for senior management? (See peer support section.)

- How can we remind ourselves and our teams about the importance of self and collective care?
- How can we support each other to implement new working practices?

5) Back to reflection

Take time to reflect on whether the integration is helpful, what could be modified, if it has not been possible to integrate the new practice – why not? Because it hasn't been helpful or because the current conditions of work do not allow it?

Self-care and collective care

What does 'self-care' mean to you? Is it a way to counteract some of the physical effects of the work or an embarrassing self-indulgence? Is it something you already do really well or something you have mixed feelings about?

Self-care is about creating and maintaining effective and appropriate boundaries. To engage in self-care requires a remembering of our inherent self-worth. Despute the popularity of the term as a sales tool for consumerism, genuine self-care can be understood as counter-cultural. Its roots are in the radical history of the fight against patriarchy, white supremacy and capitalism. We opened the book with Audre Lorde's powerful proclamation: 'Caring for myself is not self-indulgence. It is self-preservation, and that is an act of political warfare.'

Self-care is also a collective act. In fact, 'collective care' might be a better term. We cannot take care of ourselves alone or without the support and space provided by the systems we work in.

Saakvitne and Pearlman[4] answered the question 'Why practise self-care?' with the following:

- Because I hurt.
- Because I matter.
- Because my clients matter.
- Because the work I do matters.
- Because the profession matters.
- Because I must.

---

4 Saakvitne KW, Pearlman LA, Staff of TSI/CAAP, *Transforming the pain: a workbook on vicarious traumatization*, New York, NY: Norton; 1996.

The client

> No intervention that takes power away from the survivor can possibly foster her recovery, no matter how much it appears to be in her immediate best interest.[5]

Our client's best interests are the first and last rule of our work. One of the most difficult aspects of the work can be where our obligations as lawyers running a case appear to cause emotional harm to our clients.

Our duties to our firm, to the court or to conduct rules can at times feel at odds with our client's interests. Billing pressures, court timetables and other constraints also significantly affect our ability to spend the time we wish with clients. As a partner, manager or senior clerk, we have a responsibility to our colleagues to ensure that they have sustainable work into the future, not just for the ongoing viability of the organisation as a business, but because of a deep care for our colleagues and a belief in the importance of the work itself.

Yet, despite our best efforts, there are often clashes: having to chase a client about repeated reassessments for legal aid eligibility; being unable to obtain the allowances for a client's disability; explaining the financial value that the court will place on the loss of a loved one. Ultimately, we frequently have to engage in systems which we know have low levels of success for clients. Then, we are the messenger of the bad news.

Taking care of ourselves

We do this work *because our clients matter* and because we care. This is an admirable quality of those in the sector. It also can be the driving force behind the change the profession needs to address vicarious trauma. Our own wellbeing is important, but it can be hard to believe that, or prioritise it, when representing clients in the age of the 'hostile environment' and austerity. If we cannot prioritise our wellbeing for the sake of ourselves, then we can – and must – do so for the sake of our clients and our future clients.

We spend our blood, sweat and tears (sometimes literally all three when preparing urgent bundles) on becoming a lawyer and establishing our practice. Each day that we work builds our expertise and skill. If we intend to stay in the profession, we have a responsibility

---

5 Judith Herman, *Trauma and recovery: the aftermath of violence—from domestic abuse to political terror*, 1992, p133.

to our future clients to build a sustainable practice and practise good boundary-setting.

This expands to the profession as a whole. What can we do to ensure the sustainability of our profession for our future clients?

Furthermore, we are deserving of a good quality of life. We are permitted to have ease and joy in our lives. If you are reading this book, the chances are you are doing more than your fair share of social good in the world. Is it possible to feel that you have 'done enough' given your current resources?

Passion, care and drive are admirable qualities of most legal aid / social justice sector, or any lawyer who represents the interests of those in need. It also must be driving force behind the change the profession needs to address vicarious trauma.

> 'I wanted to be a . . . responsible supervisor. I tried to support my trainee to my best ability but I felt I was now exposing the next generation to harm without the proper tools. As a junior lawyer, because of power dynamics, I was so much less able to set proper boundaries. It was something I tried to keep in mind and I tried to protect her at a cost to myself as nothing was being done by people more senior than me. Sometimes you need decisions just taken out of your hands: this is what is going to happen, this is the boundary, stop.'
>
> *Solicitor*

The value of being an advocate

The research on vicarious trauma and trauma in general is predominantly conducted within the therapeutic professions. Guidance as to how best to approach work with traumatised people is usually aimed at therapists or other mental health professionals. It is vital to remember that, despite how often it may feel that way, our role is not to provide therapy to our clients. The key question is how we can be better in our roles and with our purpose as lawyers.

While we can learn from other professions, the potential for learning is mutual. Renowned trauma therapist Judith Herman is said to have been inspired in her approach to her therapeutic work with trauma survivors by the way in which lawyers created a relationship of trust in order for the client to remember the details of their case and access memories of their past.[6]

Following an extensive review of mental health recovery narratives,[7] Professor Gail Hornstein found the following factors were key to individual recovery:

1) Being listened to.
2) Being believed.
3) Having an empathic witness to their suffering.
4) Being seen by at least one key person as capable of becoming fully well.

What is particularly striking is how well the role of a lawyer, when conducted carefully and thoughtfully with adequate resources, meets those four key factors for mental health recovery.

'One thing that really struck me when I was doing crime and – in particular – pleas in mitigation, is that I would be asking a series of questions of my clients and then I would go in almost immediately to do a plea in mitigation, as they had pleaded guilty or had been found guilty. I would make these submissions, I would articulate their story, their narrative, and then go back and see them [the client] after whatever sentence they had been given and they would almost look harrowed: they would see the way I had just described their life as their life. Almost like a realisation, when I'm pulling on the strings of tribunal, that they hadn't really seen their lives in that way, that they hadn't had those opportunities. It was quite poignant, experiencing that, to see them reflecting on their life when I had been describing that to the Judge.'

Barrister

Although we do need to test our client's evidence, even in cases where our client's memory may be affected by traumatic stress, we can do so in a context where we re-inforce our belief in the client.

---

6 Appignanesi, p485.
7 Professor of Psychology at Mount Holyoke College in South Hadley, Massachusetts (US), 'Recovery: what helps and what doesn't' presented at the 3rd International Congress on Hearing Voices Savona, Italy, September 2, 2011: www.parlaconlevoci.it/pdf/savona2011/Hornstein-Savona-2011.pdf.

Resisting re-traumatisation of the client

When we work on the basis that trauma – in all its forms – is prevalent in society and that any individual we encounter (colleague or client) may have experienced trauma, we must begin to practice in ways that resist re-traumatisation of our clients.

The measures put in place will depend on the particular type of case, the environment in which we meet or interact with our clients, and will be impacted by factors beyond our control.

Steps you may want to focus on (and may already instinctively take into account) could include:

- Ensuring that we are listening carefully, to minimise the time spent re-living the incident.
- Allowing client control (as best we can) over when and how they talk about the traumatic experience.
- Explaining *why* you are asking sensitive questions.
- Taking time to establish boundaries and expectations.
- Importance of acknowledging the full experiences (even if some details are 'irrelevant' to the legal case).
- Not reinforcing the systems of power that create the abuse.
- Ensuring that the client has control or power wherever possible.
- Finding out what your client has found to help them (or harm them) when they have had to talk about the incident, and not presuming that what has been helpful for a previous client will be helpful for every client, for example
- Keeping a door open or closed / sitting near the door or sitting away from the door, facing it.
- Grounding techniques – can we help support an environment that allows the client to stay in the 'window of tolerance'? That is, the physical environment as well as the relational / psychological environment created by your relationship with the client.
- If the client's traumatic experience is not directly relevant to the case but they want to talk about it, be clear about setting boundaries for the benefit of the lawyer and client. Boundaries are not hard, harsh things but protective and supportive and an act of care.

We must also remember to remove the weight of responsibility that we may subconsciously carry for the whole of the trauma, when we are with a client who is actively traumatised by the legal process. When we take on a case, we can feel responsible for every effect. However, if the client needs to take legal action in their own best interests – while we can minimise re-traumatisation – the system itself is traumatising, so we can also acknowledge that. And, remind ourselves we did not cause the trauma.

Setting boundaries

Setting boundaries with clients is important. Setting them takes work – and so does maintaining them. We may slip and allow a boundary to be crossed, even many times. It takes work to keep establishing and maintaining boundaries with clients, being clear on what we will and will not do, what is and isn't possible. If a client has spent their life having their needs ignored, their safety threatened and their dignity violated, one way they may have responded is by developing tools that are very effective in engaging the attention and action of others. It can be helpful to understand the 'demanding' client in this broader and more compassionate way. It is not our responsibility to change the client, but setting clear boundaries is an important way to help them engage with their own legal proceedings. Equally, another client may have developed protective strategies that keep them disengaged or hard to reach (which demands our attention and resources in another way).

Some clients may swing between the two, just as our own responses to trauma do. The client in a state of hyper-arousal may seem chaotic, in need of constant reassurance, fearful and agitated in 'safe' situations or in response to straightforward correspondence. A client in a state of hypo-arousal may seem apathetic.

Both may need information repeated (as we have set out above, one of the effects of trauma is on memory and cognitive processing).

I would say I experienced vicarious trauma working on one particular case, which affected my legal practice for a while after that. At that point in my career I was at the peak of my confidence and was good at having professional boundaries, as well as being able to support my clients and develop a rapport.

This particular client was the exact same age as me. I felt I had a personal connection with her and could relate to her. It was a difficult and long-term case.

The stress crept in and I started to feel that I wasn't coping and wasn't supporting my client and I lost my understanding of boundaries and how to maintain them. Without the right support I started to take on the trauma . . . She had worked so hard to change her life around and what was happening to her was so unjust. Her mental health deteriorated dramatically. She would send me long hand-written letters, 45 pages at least, every week, and she would expect me to read them as well as dealing with my other 85–100 client caseload.

I had been mainly working on fixed fee cases and had been financially successful. This case was entirely different and no one factored in how to do this kind of case, the supervision I needed . . .

At the same time, one of my colleagues went on long-term leave and her caseload was spread out across the team. I would do more normal caseload in the working week and then focus on this particular client in the evenings and weekends when my phone wasn't ringing. I didn't appreciate that this could lead to burnout. I'd been a hard worker my entire life. I was used to working non-stop and no one was telling me not to work this way. My family and partner were in another part of the country. The firm valued the high intensity work I was doing. The hours I worked was evidence that prison law was financially viable, even though my salary was well below the living wage.

I wanted to be a good lawyer and earn a living. So I thought I just had to keep going, working hard and proving my worth, and nothing was telling me otherwise. I didn't recognise what culminated stress or possible vicarious trauma could do. This led me to carry out cases that way. It was the only way I knew to be successful. No one challenged me or thought about my wellbeing.'

Solicitor

Boundaries are not just for the 'demanding' client. A 'difficult' client is not always a traumatised client, and a traumatised client is not always a 'difficult' client! However, by setting clear boundaries we are better able to support both clients, to sustain our legal practice, and protect our quality of life.

Our individual ability to set boundaries is dependent on the environment we work in. Some questions to consider are:

- Does our supervisor model boundary-setting?
- Was this explicitly addressed in our training?
- What practices have we learnt from colleagues?
- Is this explicitly addressed in our organisation's training?
- Do you know a colleague who manages this well? Or less well?

Making a plan

It is normal and understandable to experience feelings of guilt as a result of our vicarious exposure to trauma. We may be acutely aware of our own privilege. Wallowing in our guilt is not helpful, but neither is giving too much of our time to clients and over-extending ourselves.

When we are acutely stressed or experiencing difficult emotions, it is hard to make decisions about how to best take care of ourselves, for the benefit of ourselves, our team and our clients (as well as for our loved ones).

We will face these decisions about our work-life balance on a daily basis and while there is of course an element of discretion, it can be helpful to have a clear strategy as this will take less of our cognitive and emotional resources than making each decision in the moment. This is even more true when we are experiencing acute stress or difficult emotions.

The time we invest when we are less stressed and have more capacity will benefit us when, for whatever reason, our capacity is limited.

Individual action

Overview

We will consider a number of ways that we can support ourselves on an individual level, including:

- Getting to know your early signs of stress, burnout or vicarious trauma.
- Creating regular opportunities to check-in.
- Creating safety where there is a sense of unsafety (although acknowledging that not everyone can feel totally safe in all situations).
- Reconnecting to your values.
- Regulating the nervous system.
- Replenishing your energy and motivation to fight. In the business of daily life it is all too easy to forget that self-care starts with the basics. Maintaining 'a good diet, exercise, and healthy way of life'[1] have been shown to have significant positive benefits for therapists and those working with trauma.
- Creating rituals and setting boundaries.
- Exploring ways to not add to the trauma.
- Practising mindfulness and grounding practices (examples are given throughout the book).
- Reflective writing.
- Personal therapy and other support.

This is not an exhaustive list. It's about taking the time to understand what nourishes and rebalances each person.

Window of tolerance: a tool to check-in

We set out above the window of tolerance model. It can be useful for our own reflection.

On a scale of 0–10 (10 being total hyper-arousal, 0 being total hypo-arousal, 5 being in the centre of the window of tolerance) – where are you right now?

Then, what do you need to move one place towards 5?

If we can catch ourselves at '7' or '3' it is much easier to return to the window of tolerance than if we have reached 9 or 1.

---

1 Figley, 2003 fn 28, p173.

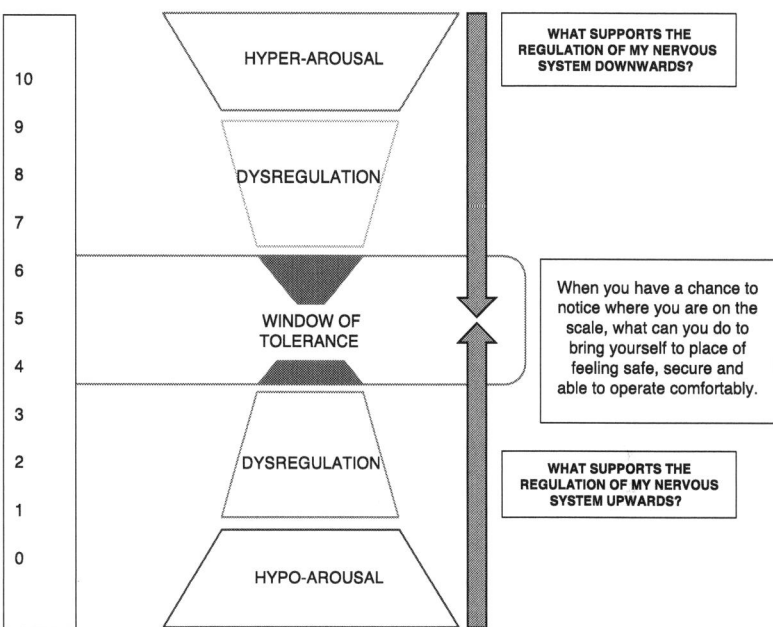

Another way of asking the question is, what would help me feel safer right now? If the body is ready to fight or flee, will going for a run or having a bubble bath support me?

These are not exhaustive or definitive lists as to what can regulate us. Some activities or practices could be useful in both roles for one person – for example, an explosive box-fit class might help discharge excess energy (down regulate) or energise us (up regulate).

What is experienced as an energising or calming activity for one person will be different for another. However, space, time and regular practice at checking how we are doing and what we might need, is key.

Rather than provide a list of activities, more important is some time and space to reflect on what we already do – we are likely using a lot of different coping strategies.

Does this take us up or down the scale? Towards or away from our window of tolerance?

Can we notice what function our activities play for us? For example, does a particular activity or coping strategy leave me feeling energised; does it quiet the mind; give a feeling of release or self-expression; or something else?

By taking notice of these effects, we are better equipped to create a more useful 'toolkit'. For example, if we do something to relieve stress that in the long-term does not make us feel better, we might recognise what benefit that activity *does* have and then consider what activity might better support sustainable wellbeing. This is also a helpful reflection if we are unable to rely on our usual self-care activities or practices (eg because of injury, illness or some other reason).

'I also try and exercise as much as possible. I run and listen to random music, so I don't have to think about anything; those moments are important. That leads me back to [finding a way not to have] to think about society's problems all the time. I try and carve out time when as much as possible I'm just not thinking about anything.'

Paralegal

Reconnecting to our values

Staying connected to our values is a protective factor against burnout and compassion fatigue. These values and motivations can change over time. The work we do, and our personal circumstances, can also change. It is therefore a useful practice to reflect from time to time, to see how.

'For a long time I felt like I owed somebody – because I'd been given something, I owed something back. I felt I had to do work that I could justify to people that I was doing good, morally responsible work. As time has gone on, I've thought a bit more about what I need and my own priorities, rather than what other people think about what I do. I'm not so worried about being judged.'

Solicitor

What values motivate your work?

For example:

- making a difference day-to-day;
- the principle of legal representation for all, equality before the law;
- equity, equality, anti-discrimination;
- spiritual, religious or political values;
- academic or intellectual challenge;
- spending time with clients face-to-face.

Is your current practice fulfilling those values?

For example, someone who is motivated by achieving concrete outcomes for their clients might be less well-suited to practice where cases take a long time to reach an outcome; or where the outcomes are focussed on financial recompense and public findings (eg inquest work).

What sustains you?

This is a slightly longer exercise to help us pay attention to our own wellbeing in a holistic way, with a focus on what is particularly important to us each individually.

1) Find time – at least 10 minutes – where you are unlikely to be disturbed and can focus on the exercise.
2) Take a blank sheet of paper and draw four lines to split the sheet into nine boxes, a little like a large hash symbol across the page: #

3) Give each box a heading from the following list – you will see that there are more than nine options, so you can choose those that are most applicable to your life:
   - ☐ health
   - ☐ sport
   - ☐ environment
   - ☐ community
   - ☐ friendships
   - ☐ family relationships
   - ☐ intimate relationships
   - ☐ work
   - ☐ spirituality / religion
   - ☐ nature
   - ☐ travel
   - ☐ creativity / art
   - ☐ personal development / growth
   - ☐ culture / heritage

4) You can also add in ones of your own, particularly if there is something missing from this list that is important to you.

5) For each box, take some time to consider *how important this aspect of your life is to you*. Assign a value out of ten (1 being not at all important, 10 being extremely important).

6) Once you have done this, take some time again to reflect on how you feel your current life is fulfilling these aspects. This is intended to be a reflection of *how things are right now*. Give this a score out of ten.

7) Then take some time to *consider the whole*. Compare the two scores for each area. Are there areas that are very important to you that are not fulfilled at the moment? Even in these times, are there ways of 'increasing the score' for that area? Can you be creative in how you do that? For example, maybe you cannot go open water swimming but maybe you could take a cold shower for that same release of adrenaline!

8) Conversely, you might find areas where you are focussing a lot of energy and time but that aren't actually your priority. For example, spending a lot of time creating a perfect looking environment in your home, but missing a sense of spirituality or connection to your religion. Is it possible to shift some of the time or resource spent on one to find more fulfilment in the other?

This exercise is designed to be repeated as often as is helpful. It is a snapshot of a moment in time, rather than a fixed document. In this way, it is a kind of 'mindfulness of my values' practice. Noticing the core values that guide your life, and paying careful attention to how these things are for you in this moment.

Individual practices

Specific rituals or practices can be helpful to provide boundaries between your work and non-work life, and before and after client meetings or handling traumatic material. For example:

- Handwashing: At the time of writing, this has new significance and we are likely doing a lot more than before. However, can the handwashing before/after an encounter with a client or time in court or the police station be a moment of quiet reflection, marking the boundaries between each part of our day?
- Having a work 'uniform': Whole outfit, or just an emblematic part eg jacket, tie, tying hair back, brooch – a spider brooch a la Lady Hale, for example?[2]
- Setting out and packing up your workspace each day.
- Listening to music or a podcast on the way to or from work as a mental demarcation.

What other opportunities are there in your day?

These practices can also become helpful subconscious indicators for the nervous system that a particular event is 'over' and (absent any other ongoing threat) allowing it to return towards homeostasis.

Don't add to the trauma

What can we do to minimise exposure to trauma?

It is certainly not always possible to limit our exposure to trauma. This will depend on the workplace structures and our personal circumstances. Some examples are given below.

---

2 S Conlon, 'How Lady Hale's giant spider brooch sent the web into a spin', *The Guardian*, 28 September 2019: www.theguardian.com/fashion/2019/sep/28/ lady-hale-spider-brooch-launches-global-trend.

At work

- Feel confident to say 'not now' to a colleague who wants to discuss a difficult case if you are feeling at your capacity (see section on debriefing, below).
- Set time limits on engaging with difficult content where possible.
- Consider co-working particular cases to share the load of reviewing traumatic material.
- Implement a policy of using content warnings when sending documents between colleagues.

At home

- Give yourself permission not to keep up-to-date with the news.
- Set limits on social media use.
- Check for content warnings on television shows or films.
- Acknowledge that listening to the worries and trauma of friends and family may be adding to the load, and consider how boundaries can be set in these contexts too.

> 'It is difficult if you try to switch off . . . You are thinking, "why am I watching trashy TV when I could be helping someone?" But you can't do that 24 hours per day!'
>
> *Paralegal*

Reflective writing practice

Reflective practice can be enhanced by including writing as part of the reflection. Lawyers often enjoy words and process concepts linguistically, so a regular writing practice can be a helpful tool if that is the case.

Questions for reflection

You might want to use some of the questions within this book as prompts, or use writing practice, as set out below.

Writing practice[3]

Reflective writing practice

Answering questions in a structured way, focussing on thoughts, feelings and perhaps using a set format for regular check-in.

Free writing?[4]

Free writing is often thought of as a creative writing tool. It can also be a useful tool for reflection or as an alternative form of mindfulness practice (for more on this read Natalie Goldberg's classic *Writing down the bones*[5]).

- Set a particular goal – either the time you will write for (say, between 10 and 30 minutes) *or* the number of pages (this will depend on how you are writing but if by hand on A4, then between one and three sides).
- Try writing by hand if possible.
- Try to do this at the same time every day.
- Write! The only task is to start writing and not to stop. Word after word, like a stream of consciousness.
- There is no need to quality control, and try not to edit yourself at all. You do not have to write beautifully, it does not need to make sense or be grammatically correct. If you run out of things to write you can write 'I don't know what to write' over and over again until something else comes in.
- These pages are not to be read by anyone. They can be shredded, thrown away, or saved if you wish. If you want to read them back, try waiting at least a month before reading back. If you are worried about someone else reading them, you can write a line and then write your second line over the top, then start a new line and write over that one.
- Like sitting meditation, sometimes it feels like we're dredging up the most annoying negative parts of our mind. Or we find blankness, or frantic energy, or it is very dull. Whatever it is, we let it out (and let it go). If you can, try it for two weeks every day. If it is

---

3 Obviously we need to consider privacy and data protection and for these practices to be effective there is no need to include any client details.

4 Inspired by Natalie Goldberg, *Writing down the bones: freeing the writer within,* Shambhala Publications Inc, 2005; and Julia Cameron, *The artist's way: a course in discovering and recovering your creative self,* Macmillan, 2016.

5 Natalie Goldberg, *Writing down the bones: freeing the writer within,* Shambhala Publications Inc, 2005.

helpful, continue. It might not feel helpful straightaway, but with time can be very powerful, which is why we recommend giving it a go for a little while.

Personal therapy and other individual help

It might be the case that the negative effects of work (and/or pressures from your personal life) mean that additional personal support is necessary. There are several potential channels of support within the legal profession, including:

- LawCare has a free and confidential helpline and webchat.[6] LawCare also provides information and support on mental health and wellbeing issues for those who work in the legal profession and their families.[7]
- Wellbeing at the Bar[8] provides barristers and chambers' personnel with the information and skills they need in order to try and stay well.

Outside of the legal profession, lawyers should be encouraged to access any other relevant support to deal with the mental health effects of the work.

- Your GP may be able to refer you for a range of talking therapies or prescribe medication.
- Mindfulness-based interventions (mindfulness-based cognitive therapy (MBCT), mindfulness-based stress reduction (MBSR), acceptance and commitment therapy (ACT) programmes) are available through the NHS and privately.
- There are some trauma-specific treatments available on the NHS, depending on availability in your area (for example, trauma-focused cognitive behavioural therapy (CBT) or eye movement desensitisation and reprocessing (EMDR)) and whether the referral criteria are met.
- Some employees will have the use of 'employee assistance programmes' (EAPs) through their employer. It may be worth checking what is available through these and if there are any trauma-informed services available.

---

6 See: www.lawcare.org.uk/helpline. Helpline 0800 279 6888 Monday–Friday 9am–5.30pm. Live chat Monday and Wednesday 1.15–5.30pm, Thursday 9am–1.15pm. Email support@lawcare.org.uk.

7 See: www.lawcare.org.uk/about-us/what-we-do.

8 See: www.wellbeingatthebar.org.uk/.

- Private therapy may not be affordable for all (although there are low-cost services available, particularly through organisations that train counsellors and psychotherapists) but can be extremely beneficial, particularly where in-work support is not available.

> 'Going to see [a] therapist was really helpful . . . I wasn't earning a lot of money and still paying back my LPC loan so it was not a small amount for my circumstances. I saw her for a good few months and found it really useful.'
>
> *Solicitor*

More resources are set out in appendix B.

CHAPTER 10

Team and peer action

Staff support is not a luxury but a necessity.[1] There are a variety of measures that can be implemented at the team and peer level, which can be adapted to the wide range of circumstances in which lawyers work. We will set out a number of differing types:

– Peer support

– Supervision

– Debriefing

Figley, 2003

Many social justice lawyers will be familiar with this scenario:

You meet your (non-lawyer) friends on a Friday evening after a particularly stressful working week. At some point, perhaps after you have had something to eat, relaxed, or had a drink or two, someone asks how work is going. You throw out a few details of the kinds of cases you have been working on without thinking too much and realise your friends are looking at you in horror. Your 'everyday' kind of case sounds like an unthinkable set of events to them. Conversely, dependent on their work, you may feel that their 'stressful' day may not match the severity and intensity of yours or your clients'. It can feel as if the only people who understand are your fellow colleagues and peers.

This scenario chimes with the anecdotal and research evidence on the empowering impact of peer support, sometimes described as 'debriefing'. From our interviews – even in work places where those structures are not formally in place – practitioners have informally sought them out by speaking with colleagues. Or, they have pointed to the absence of peer support as something that they actively want, for themselves or their team.

> 'I think that confidential peer support is really important . . . I think having perspective and seeing other people's experiences; peer support is just about understanding that . . . I don't see that as something that is available for more senior practitioners . . . Some kind of structure that allows senior managers to share good or poor practice in a safe place would be beneficial. It's about the stresses of managing people, because you have got other people's lives in your hands and they are the lifeline for your clients in the future as well. Peer support is a very

---

1 Figley, 2003, fn 28, p171.

specific thing and I think something similar for more senior practitioners to have an opportunity to support and mentor each other, would be really good. I am very lucky in own personal set up that I currently feel able to absorb the cumulative stress of those I support, but I don't think everyone is in that position.'

Solicitor

'I am very thankful to have really good co-workers. I tend to just speak about how I am finding a particular case stressful or a particular situation stressful. I find it is quite good to bounce off others in the same situation. It is also about finding other avenues to manage that stress . . . It was good to meet with like-minded people and again talk about similar experiences and what kind of strategies people had in place to manage that.'

Solicitor

Peer support

What is peer support?

Peer support is a system of giving and receiving help founded on key principles of respect, shared responsibility, and mutual agreement of what is helpful. Peer support is not based on psychiatric models and diagnostic criteria. It is about understanding another's situation empathically through the shared experience of emotional and psychological pain.[2]

At its simplest, peer support is the exchange of support between people who have something in common. It is a model that features heavily in community-based strategies to improve mental health and wellbeing both formally facilitated by charities, non-governmental organisations (NGOs) and self-help groups; and informally through service-users sharing their experiences with one another. Peer support forms part of the government's mental health outcomes

2 Mind (2013). 'Mental health peer support in England: piecing together the jigsaw' available at www.mind.org.uk/media/5910954/piecing-together-the-jigsaw-full-version.pdf, quoting Shery Mead (2003) 'Defining peer support' available at http://chrysm-associates.co.uk/images/SMeadDefiningPeerSupport.pdf.

strategy 'No health without mental health'[3] and is a tool used for mental health professionals (eg the Balint method[4]). However, it is notably absent as a consistent structure of support and resilience within the legal field.

The anecdotal evidence is supported by clear evidence of the positive impact of peer support in the mental health sector:

> As mental health service users we take each other's stories seriously where often the professionals do not. Telling our stories and listening to each other's stories is the cornerstone of peer support, empowerment and recovery. But it is also a political act.
>
> Faulkner and Basset, 2010[5]

> The mutuality and reciprocity that occurs through peer support builds social capital, which in turn is associated with well-being and resilience.
>
> McKenzie, 2006

The power of peer support cannot be overstated.[6] It involves the bringing together of a group of people with shared working practices, shared pressures and a shared endeavour to achieve the best for their clients despite the enormity of the challenges presented by the current climate. Quite literally, it is a structure that allows you to access the support of your peers.

It is possibly an even more important tool for lawyers because it can be developed informally (in absence of structural measures in place across the profession) and can be contained within the boundaries of colleagues to avoid breaching client confidentiality.

---

3   *No health without mental health: implementation framework*, Department of Health, 2012, available at: www.gov.uk/government/publications/ mental-health-implementation-frameworkhttps://www.gov.uk/government/ publications/mental-health-implementation-framework at 4.26.

4   See The Balint Society: https://balint.co.uk.

5   Mind, 2013.

6   Strong support for this can be found in, Yael Fischman, PhD, 'Secondary trauma in the legal professions, a clinical perspective', *TORTURE*, Volume 18, Number 2, 2008, pp112–114.

'The things that distress us are often the key aspects of the case; sometimes that granular understanding of the issues, the distress, is really helpful. When the distress is from client work rather than pressure and volume, you cannot really deal with it unless you have been there and seen it. That sharing process has been the most important thing.'

Solicitor

While some practitioners do this informally, having a formal structure readily available can be preferable: it ensures that the level of support available is not conditional on your position in an organisation, the resources of your organisation or the working schedule and commitments of a friend or colleague.

Looking at the two options together allows the pros and cons of each approach to be properly considered. We acknowledge that much will depend on the needs and resources of your peers and your organisation. Peer support can be between just two or three people or a bigger group.

Informal peer support

Pros

- Flexibility.
- You can choose a buddy or group within work that you trust and feel safe sharing with.
- Peers may understand situations better than someone in a different role.
- A few minutes to complain about an unfair situation, to vent about a difficult opponent or client, or to share the horror of the facts of a particular case, may be sufficient to discharge some of the emotional effect to get back to work.
- It can help create a supportive workplace environment in which people who are struggling get help and support earlier, and where people recognise the 'warning signs'.
- It is responsive to more immediate need after a particular event.

Cons

- We do not always have the right peers or colleagues to meet our needs.
- Working remotely or from home (as – at the time of writing – we now all are) we may miss the more natural way this can unfold.
- The debriefing can perpetuate the trauma by spreading it to the listener – see the concept of 'sliming' in the Debrief section below.[7]
- Risks of miscommunication; discrimination; centring of those who complain loudest. For example, a white lawyer working on a race discrimination case may offload to a Black colleague about the specific facts of case in a way that is blind to the potential effects on that colleague; or discussing the details of a particular type of abuse, injury or illness of which a colleague has personal and distressing experience, and of which the colleague who is offloading is not aware.

Formal peer support (or debriefing)

Pros

- Being scheduled in gives the space importance and a sense of priority.
- It ensures that practitioners have a regular chance for reflection (see the section on reflective practice).
- This can be with peers, with a more experienced lawyer, or an external clinical supervisor. (or someone equally experienced if senior), a chance to learn good practice from someone who is likely to have experienced something similar. With a clinical supervisor, a chance for a confidential therapeutic relationship with a skilled listener.

Cons

- Planned at specific times, so may mean waiting for some time after a particularly difficult or triggering event.
- Can be dependent on a good relationship with a supervisor or other professional.
- It can be resource intensive. Within legal supervision you are dependent on the time and availability of a senior lawyer and it takes time away from billable work for both parties. With externally facilitated peer support and suitable professional clinical supervi-

---

7 Françoise Mathieu.

sion there is a cost (although it is worth noting that the hourly rate for a suitable mental health professional is unlikely to exceed the rate for a senior solicitor who might otherwise manage a peer support session).

- Needs to be supported within the workplace or can be squeezed out.
- Barristers do not have a readily-available structure.

> 'I have worked in another role . . . when studying the BPTC . . . it was a big team. What we did to manage the stress of a hearing was to have regular meetings where we would discuss what had gone wrong, no one was angry or stressed, we would just talk together, work out a solution, act on the solution, and then it would be resolved. Experiencing that level of efficiency in relation to a problem was amazing. If you tackle an issue head on as a unit, then it will no longer be a stress, it will be resolved. I think working as a team and communicating properly with everyone in a team is key. When you work together you are not [likely to be] stressed and burnout.'
>
> *Pupil barrister*

Supervision

Legal supervision (by a senior legal colleague)

Alongside the regular, formal, legal supervision of specific cases or caseload, these meetings are an opportunity for supervisors to check-in on a 'pastoral' basis. Difficulties with progress on cases; outstanding WIP and chargeable time; or with particular clients, may be indicators of more general difficulties or may be exacerbated by the psychological impact of the work. Often however, with the pressures of work on both sides, little to no time may be allowed for checking in with the supervisee's wellbeing.

It is unfortunately not uncommon across the profession for supervision to be brief, infrequent, poor quality or for it to not happen at all.

Regardless of the possibility of a non-legal supervision, the 'traditional' form of supervision is an important part of a lawyer's management of their caseload and time which is crucial in the management of the risk of burnout.

Non-legal supervision

Group supervision

One form of non-legal, or 'clinical' supervision involves bringing in a mental health practitioner to facilitate small groups for group therapy or reflection. In many ways it is similar to the peer support but instead can also be a therapeutic space, rather than simply a reflective space. It has the advantage of allowing lawyers access to an independent and trained third-party, at lower cost than one-to-one supervision, with some of the benefit of formal peer support.

Individual supervision

The 'gold-standard' for psychological support is the provision of a properly trained mental health professional (likely a counsellor or psychotherapist), ideally with relevant experience, providing one-to-one support on a regular basis to all employees exposed to traumatic material in the course of their work.

> 'It was a way of offloading in a way that didn't provoke a defensive reaction from an employer. It was a neutral space. I was able to explore why certain things affected me more than others and why I was feeling a certain way towards some clients. Part of the difficulty is that sometimes your clients are just not that attractive [as people or personalities] and you find yourself thinking horrible things but there is no way to discuss that at work. It was a way to deal with my own emotions about the work and to recognise that it is ok to have complex feelings about this stuff.'
>
> *Solicitor*

In many professions, such as clinical psychology or psychotherapy, clinical supervision is a compulsory part of the role.

The time would be allowed for within working hours, on a totally confidential basis. The frequency of the sessions would likely depend on the type of work and context of each employee and organisation. Extra support could be offered, including to those who do not take up the offer of regular supervision, in the event of an acutely traumatic incident (eg the death of a client in traumatic circumstances, assault or threatened assault by a client or witness, etc).

It is possible to have an arrangement whereby persistent and common issues within the particular workplace could be raised by the supervisor – where it is possible to do so without identifying any particular individual. This may not be possible, particularly in smaller organisations, but there are other ways of ensuring that there is productive, honest and safe feedback throughout the organisation.

The above is distinct from private counselling, albeit the type of professional engaged would be the same or similar. It may be appropriate for a firm to pay for an employee to receive private counselling, out of work hours and off premises. Those organisations with 'employee assistance programmes' (EAPs) may have this included in their package. However, in these cases it is unlikely to be appropriately tailored to the unique work of a social justice lawyer.

'Even just having a chat with someone who was approaching it from a therapeutic angle rather talking to another stressed-out lawyer who takes a lawyer's approach, was really helpful. He put me in touch with a therapist who I started seeing once a month.

I told my employers about it and I really believe it is something that should be in place for lawyers. It is an outgoing for the firm and a lot of practices don't feel they have the money to do it, but they then end up losing people.'

Associate solicitor

'It is really important that – whoever you work for – if you are dealing with clients or areas of work that are traumatic, if the client is vulnerable or there is abuse involved (there are a whole range of factors that could make it traumatic) – support should be offered to you by your employer. That support can either be one on one, by telephone, or whatever means is available, but it has to be something that you can get either anonymously or confidentially. I have had that offered to me in one role and it was really positive. It also meant that everyone in the team was able to speak to someone if they needed to. I think that was a really good way of managing and supporting people who are working in areas of trauma.'

Pupil barrister

It is important – in this context – to recognise the impact of supervision in and of itself. This is well-recognised as a fundamental component of the work of therapists.

> 'Much secondary trauma can be avoided or its effects ameliorated if therapists seek regular supervision or consultation' (Cerney, 1995, p. 139). Pearlman and McCann (1990) stressed the importance of regular supervision or consultation when working with crime victims or survivors of other traumas. The purpose of this is to process the painful client material, as well as any personal emotions or cognitions (Cerney, 1995) that may be experienced as overwhelming. This is a vital process in preventing STS.[8]

> Figley, 2003

Debriefing

After a particularly difficult incident – for instance the death of a client; violence or threatened violence during work – debriefing is of paramount importance. However, the need can also arise from more common incidents, such as difficult telephone calls with clients who might be in extreme distress. This debriefing must also be complemented by training on how to manage these incidents in the first place.

Casework supervisors have a clear and important role. It may be more appropriate for a different person to manage and/or be trained in specific non-legal debriefing of team members that they manage. For example, this role could be adopted by someone in the HR team (where available and subject to the need for them to have a specific understanding of the needs and pressures on practitioners); training principals; a particular partner; or chambers committee members.

> 'All aspects of client care should be so much more of a focus. It should not be something you learn on the job – I feel so strongly about this – everyone has different social skills. We got given a worksheet for someone who is suicidal, but that's it. What about the grieving mothers that we speak to two weeks after their son's death?'
>
> *Paralegal*

---

8 Yael Fischman, PhD, 'Secondary trauma in the legal professions, a clinical perspective', *TORTURE*, Volume 18, Number 2, 2008, pp112–114.

How to debrief effectively[9]

We usually have little or no control over how or when a client or witness tells us the details of the story, from the first person to answer the phone, to meeting outside the courtroom door. However, we do have control over how or when we engage with and debrief with our colleagues.

Experienced counsellor and Compassion Fatigue specialist, Françoise Mathieu provides a vivid alternative way of understanding the structural and social aspect of trauma at an organisational level and what this means for how we communicate within organisations.

> The main problem ... is that the listener, the recipient of the traumatic details, rarely has a choice in receiving this information. Therefore, they are being slimed rather than taking part in a debriefing process. Therein lies the problem and the solution.[10]

As a profession, we often feel desensitised to the details of traumatic cases, particularly stories that are common in our field of work. Desensitisation might be helpful in many respects. If we can find ourselves feeling the negative effects of trauma, it makes sense that we would develop strategies to block out any of the negative feelings. However, the lack of feeling in the moment does not mean we are not affected by it. The effect can be cumulative. The same is true for our colleagues.

> Low-impact debriefing is a simple and easy VT protection strategy. It aims to sensitize helpers to the impact that sharing graphic details can have on themselves and on their colleagues.[11]

Mathieu's 'low impact debriefing'

A note on the steps

These steps were formulated in the therapy world where there may be more structure to a working day and a culture in which this kind of conversation feels more natural and is more easily included. It

---

9 We are indebted to the model of Françoise Mathieu: 'Low impact debriefing: preventing retraumatization, 31 May 2013: www.tendacademy.ca/low-impact-debriefing-how-to-stop-sliming-each-other/; and *The Compassion Fatigue Workbook: Creative Tools for Transforming Compassion Fatigue and Vicarious Traumatization*, Routledge, 2012.

10 Françoise Mathieu.

11 Mathieu, p45.

may be something that can be implemented between colleagues or peers by agreement in a formal or informal way.

Fair warning and consent

In a formal clinical supervision debrief, the practitioner will be prepared to hear a traumatic story. However, in workplace discussion we might swing from talking about a broken photocopier to something very upsetting. It is good practice to:

1) Consider the setting

- Are you at work in a quiet space where no-one can overhear you?
- Are you with a colleague at a social occasion?

2) Give the listener fair warning

Let your colleague know that you would like to 'offload' about something difficult.

3) Before speaking, ask for consent

Check that this is a good time, making it clear that you'd like to talk about a difficult case or client with them.

Only *informed* consent is *true* consent. We may already be aware of particular triggers for us. If that is not clear yet, developing a reflective practice will help us identify if there are particular case facts that will trigger difficult reactions in us. A regular reflective practice will also help us notice if particular life events increase or change those triggers.

The listener can then check that the content is something that they feel safe to hear. Our colleagues may have very deliberately chosen the area of work in which they specialise and do not undertake specific types of cases for a personal reason.

Limited disclosure

Imagine the worst details are at the centre of a spiral, decreasing in intensity on the way out to the edges. When you start to debrief, begin at the edges (with the least traumatic information) and move slowly towards the centre. You may find that you do not need to discuss all of the detail of the traumatic incident to gain the benefit from talking about it– thus saving your colleague from an unnecessary 'sliming'.

Questions for reflection

- Do you tend offload to colleagues, including the graphic details of cases?
- Do you tend to be the team or office listener?
- Do you passively absorb the details of others' caseloads?
- Do you actively seek out discussion about cases?
- How intentional is your sharing?
- Could you apply these steps to your 'offloading' outside of work?

Organisational action

When considering burnout, compassion fatigue, and vicarious traumatization, organizational factors are key. Unmanageable caseloads and work tasks, little social support, long work hours, and insufficient job-related resources are frequently cited as primary factors that enhance the likelihood that an individual will experience stress-related symptoms.

Zwisohn, Handley, Winters, Reiter[1]

It may be seen to be a 'cop-out' for legal firms to promote well-being programmes, while encouraging their staff to work long hours or have high billing requirements or caseloads. It should therefore be stressed that if a practitioner is struggling with burnout or other negative emotional consequences associated from doing asylum work, while self-care strategies are useful, it may be more beneficial to lessen their workload and their exposure to traumatized people of traumatic narratives, than to place the burden on to them to take additional tasks on, like committing themselves to exercise programmes or mindfulness classes.

Rønning, Blumberg and Dammeyer, 2020[2]

Training

Training on how to deal with trauma, traumatised clients and the impact on us as lawyers (and humans) is essential.

The importance of this kind of training cannot be overstated, particularly when one considers experiences of the extreme unpreparedness of junior lawyers when entering this field of work. The risk to clients of mismanaged or unmanaged trauma disclosure is humanly and personally profound; the risk to practitioners, no less; and, the risk to firms of negligence in respect of staff care or the management of information-gathering for clients involved in life-changing cases, a very real concern.

---

1   'Vicarious trauma in public service lawyering: how chronic exposure to trauma affects the brain and body', Megan Zwisohn, Wayne Handley, Danielle Winters, Alyssa Reiter, *Richmond Public Interest Law Review*, Volume 22, Issue 2 Article 9, p287.

2   Line Rønning, Jocelyn Blumberg and Jesper Dammeyer, 'Vicarious traumatisation in lawyers working with traumatised asylum seekers: a pilot study', *Psychiatry, Psychology and Law*, 2020.

CW: suicide

'I think my main shock with this work – I always knew this was going to be a particularly emotive area: it is inherently so where there are deaths at difficult times – but I was shocked with the lack of training around different aspects of this kind of work.

I think on my first day at my last job – it was not an inquest case, but an assault case in prison – I was sent on my own to prison to take a witness statement from someone in prison. I was not given much direction on who client was, or even how a prison works. I had no idea what was expected of me, or how it would be in the cells.

In my first week at this job I was tasked with taking a whole family's witness statements in relation to a self-inflicted death in their family. I had no training on how to deal with extremely vulnerable, emotional clients who have never been asked such direct questions in their life.

I think I am quite a hardy person, I am good at dealing with those things, but it was shocking not to be given any training in client care, and further for none of the fee earners to consider or ask after my wellbeing. It's a side of the law that is neglected. Such a key skill: social skills, it's completely amiss.'

Paralegal

The research is clear that training is a core part of effective management of traumatic caseloads:

> The most frequently found strategies included the use of peer support, supervision and consultation, training, personal therapy, maintaining balance in one's life, and setting clear limits and boundaries with clients. In addition, the study determined the existence of lasting positive changes, which had not been addressed in the literature at that time.[3]

It is, as we have set out above, a fact that we attend to our work as lawyers, but also as empathic human beings. How to manage the apparent tension that arises between these two roles and parts of our selves, when no training is delivered on: the fact that the work will be traumatic and impactful, or on how to manage that impact, is deeply troubling.

3 Fn 28, p169.

The risks to practitioners of inadequate training on how to handle traumatic material are borne out starkly in the research and are a cause of significant concern:

> Lawyers are not traditionally trained to address work-related emotions or acknowledge the potentially traumatic impact that their work may have on them and, by extension, on their clients. In some instances, they may feel overwhelmed by unidentified emotions. Continued distress may even lead them to abandon work with victims, thus depriving from legal representation an already underserved population.[4]

How is the workplace configured?

Physical configuration

At its most basic, this can simply be the layout of the office. The appropriateness of different set-ups will vary, organisation to organisation. Reflection is needed by managers and supervisors about the pinch-points for different teams, levels of staff members, and those with particularly traumatic tasks eg those that cover helplines or have to repeatedly handle 'frontline' experiences of trauma by taking witness statements. It is vital that support staff are also included in these considerations. Particular attention will need to be given to how this can be developed post COVID-19 pandemic.

'The layout of the office is very positive: it's open plan and good in that sense. But it is hard to have a moment to yourself.

It's nice having open plan: there is no hierarchy with partners locked in their offices, but equally it means that it is hard if you are having a stressful moment . . . There is nothing built in to have a moment to just breathe or – if you have read something horrible – to be by yourself and just process it.

There is simply no space for that to happen or it would be obvious if you were quite upset or just walked out of the office.'

Paralegal

---

4 Yael Fischman, PhD, 'Secondary trauma in the legal professions, a clinical perspective', *TORTURE*, Volume 18, Number 2, 2008, p109.

Case-working configuration

Attention can and should be given to case-working best practice. There are simple options available to help manage the burden of traumatic content, for example co-working or buddying schemes. This can have a powerful impact on the ability of – especially junior – practitioners to share and manage the traumatic load of their work.

> 'Setting up mechanisms that enable casework to be shared so that the practitioners that I supervise are not alone with an individual case. The cases are co-worked, which means nobody just has to read and deal and absorb in isolation, the tragic circumstances of their client. That has probably been the single most helpful response [to issues of stress, burnout and vicarious trauma in the workplace].'
>
> *Solicitor*

Similarly, open-door policies, secure and open feedback loops for issues with cases, and the time and opportunity to identify the stressors of particular files or materials, are very important.

> 'Or, taking an extra step with a case, for example, asking a practitioner to highlight in a psychological document the areas that distress them, and then share that with me.'
>
> *Solicitor*

A natural corollary of these protective steps is that it should lessen the load on managers. It is readily accepted that managing a highly stressed, burn out or vicariously traumatised workforce will be exhausting.

'When I was a newer solicitor I was a bit better at taking care of myself. As pressure the and targets increased, that went down-hill . . . As time went on and as I got more responsibility, I felt completely squeezed. I didn't get any reductions in my chargeable hours or financial targets when I had people to supervise. I was encouraged to apply to be an associate but there was no payrise and I was expected to manage people with no more money or time to do it properly. I was supervising a trainee and I wanted to give her a good training experience as well as be a responsible supervisor.'

Solicitor

It also provides a practical way for managers to take proactive steps to manage trauma, on a personal and organisational level. In our experience, this can be a great relief for the organisation.

From the lawyers we interviewed, we received the following suggestions:

- An environment where it is considered ok to fail and that support will be provided.
- More community and less hierarchy.
- Stronger supervision, with a focus on staff, their wellbeing and needs, rather than just billing and tasks.
- Adjustment or reduction of targets where a practitioner has supervision responsibilities.
- Better boundary-setting, with senior staff leading by example.
- Providing work mobiles, so practitioners do not have to use personal phones for work matters.
- Mandatory training courses on vicarious trauma.
- Availability of one-to-one counselling.

Profession-wide action

Unhealed trauma acts like a rock thrown into a pond; it causes ripples that move outward, affecting many other bodies over time. After months or years, unhealed trauma can appear to become part of someone's personality. Over even longer periods of time, as it is passed on and gets compounded through other bodies in a household, it can become a family norm. And if it gets transmitted and compounded through multiple families and generations, it can start to look like culture.[1]

Menakem

What responsibility does the legal system have to its participants?

This is a fraught question. The justice system has – in various contexts – been described as 'at breaking point' for many years.[2] Funding cuts to HM Courts and Tribunals Service (HMCTS), legal aid, and the failure to raise fixed fees for casework in line with inflation (or at all), has left the system grossly under-resourced and highly fatigued.

Protective steps

However, the development of policies that seek to integrate the protective steps set out above for individuals, teams and organisations, can also be done at a system level.

By way of example, a solicitor or legal executive instructing a barrister can adopt a good practice policy of including trigger-warnings where there is graphic content or description of traumatic incidents with a brief note as to what kind of content it is. The Crown Prosecution Service (CPS) can do the same.

Training

We would argue that training at all levels of the justice system is needed on stress, burnout and vicarious trauma and that this should be provided automatically and systematically, for:

- Judiciary.
- Court staff.
- Law students.

1   Resmaa Menakem, *My Grandmother's hands: racialized trauma and the pathway to mending our hearts and bodies*, Central Recovery Press, 2017.
2   Owen Bowcott, 'Legal aid cuts have left family courts "at breaking point"', *The Guardian*, 29 July 2014: www.theguardian.com/law/2014/jul/29/legal-aid-family-courts-breaking-point-lawyers.

- Trainee lawyers: This should be incorporated into vocational training and should include managing traumatised clients and achieving best evidence. That necessarily means taking steps to avoid re-traumatising clients or traumatising the professional who is – for example – taking a trauma-based witness statement.
- Support staff: This includes all staff who might have exposure to clients or casework, including reception, administrative, IT and costs draftspeople.
- Managers / supervisors: This is key to the effective management of organisational trauma and employee burnout.
- Current practitioners: This catches those who are embedded in traumatic work now, but would benefit from an awareness of and strategies to manage the ongoing impact of that work.
- Other organisations and practitioners: For example, the Legal Aid Agency (LAA).

'All profit-making organisations at the very least should be making proper regular provision for supervision. Had that been there throughout my career there is a chance I wouldn't have chosen to leave. It is really important to be able to talk to someone neutral, who doesn't have a vested interested in you working too many hours.'

Solicitor

Further ideas

From the lawyers we interviewed, we received the following suggestions:

- Compulsory modules on vocational training courses covering relevant issues for lawyers working with vulnerable and traumatised people, burnout and self-care.
- Regulatory and/or LAA requirement for contracts for fee earners to have regular, non-legal supervision available to them.
- Provide personal development and training on safeguarding and boundaries.

'I now work in the charity sector and I don't think that the legal sector is good enough on training in terms of boundaries or safeguarding, compared to what you have to do in the charity sector. I never had any training on that in my legal career.'

Casework consultant

- Proper review of expectations placed on junior and support staff to ensure that the lowest paid in the profession are not carrying the load in respect of vicarious trauma.

Peer support should become an accepted and encouraged part of legal practice, at each level of practitioners and for each type of practitioner. We can and should offer a wealth of experience, empathy and knowledge to one another as fellow practitioners.

There should also be space for novel ideas – for example, the idea proposed by one interviewee for compulsory breaks after traumatic cases:

> 'There should be a rule (obviously it's difficult as self-employed people), but there should be a rule, that if you do 5 day case or over or do a bolt-on case [a case involving particular complexity, sensitivity or length] . . . you have time out for a day, you are not allowed to work.
>
> If we're talking about safety and how to safely do your work. If you qualify for one of them [the length of case or bolt-ons], you have got to take a day off and [/ or] not do a trial where one of those bolt-ons applies.
>
> Without that, the nature of the vocation, the fact you're self-employed, that you don't know when your next brief will come, people will work.
>
> You don't want to let people down, you don't want to let solicitors down, you don't want to let your client down.
>
> It is almost more stressful to let them down, so you forego your own needs because it becomes more stressful if you returned the work or you did force that day off that you know that you need.
>
> I think we are never going to regulate ourselves in the way that we should because I think the role – our role as self-employed barristers – counters that regulation.'
>
> *Barrister*

While on the face of it, a potentially controversial or unmanageable approach, this advocates for specific, formalised recognition of the impact of certain types of cases. It stresses that practitioner safety demands space and time for recuperation, rest, and decompression, all of which is essential to our longevity in the profession.

Next steps

We hope and intend that this book marks the beginning (or for some, the continuation) of a renewed focus on trauma-informed working practices and collective self-care. We want practitioners to have the language and the courage to speak about the impact of this work, and to work together – whether at a team, organisational, or profession-wide level – to push for change, support and training. In writing this book, we have endeavoured to provide that language, and to inspire honest conversations between colleagues and co-workers.

As outlined at the start of this book, our ultimate goal is to ensure that the most vulnerable in society are helped by lawyers who are well-supported to deal with stress, vicarious trauma and burnout. Achieving this goal will take time and effort, regularly and consistently; there are no quick fixes. We believe that this time and this effort is incredibly important. This work matters; we matter; our clients matter. Shifting the focus onto safe, sustainable, and reflective working practices is critical to our longevity in the profession and to the sustainability of the profession as a whole.

Professional quality of life scale (ProQOL)[1]

Compassion satisfaction and compassion fatigue (ProQOL) version 5 (2009)

When you represent people you have direct contact with their lives. As you may have found, your compassion for those you represent can affect you in positive and negative ways. Below are some questions about your experiences, both positive and negative, as a lawyer.

Consider each of the following questions about you and your current work situation. Select the number that honestly reflects how frequently you experienced these things in the *last 30 days*.

1–ever	2=Rarely	3=Sometimes	4=Often	5=Very Often

____1.   I am happy.
____2.   I am preoccupied with more than one person I represent.
____3.   I get satisfaction from being able to represent people.
____4.   I feel connected to others.
____5.   I jump or am startled by unexpected sounds.
____6.   I feel invigorated after working with those I represent.
____7.   I find it difficult to separate my personal life from my life as a lawyer.
____8.   I am not as productive at work because I am losing sleep over traumatic experiences of a person I represent.
____9.   I think that I might have been affected by the traumatic stress of those I represent.
____10. I feel trapped by my job as a lawyer.

---

1   © B Hudnall Stamm, 2009–2012. Professional Quality of Life: Compassion Satisfaction and Fatigue Version 5 (ProQOL). www.proqol.org. This test may be freely copied as long as (a) author is credited, (b) no changes are made, and (c) it is not sold. Those interested in using the test should visit www.proqol.org to verify that the copy they are using is the most current version of the test. This measure is available for free in multiple languages on the website.

____11.   Because of my work as a lawyer, I have felt 'on edge' about various things.

____12.   I like my work as a lawyer.

____13   I feel depressed because of the traumatic experiences of the people I represent.

____14.   I feel as though I am experiencing the trauma of someone I have represented.

____15.   I have beliefs that sustain me.

____16.   I am pleased with how I am able to keep up with legal techniques and protocols.

____17.   I am the person I always wanted to be.

____18.   My work makes me feel satisfied.

____19.   I feel worn out because of my work as a lawyer.

____20.   I have happy thoughts and feelings about those I represent and how I could help them.

____21.   I feel overwhelmed because my caseload seems endless.

____22.   I believe I can make a difference through my work.

____23.   I avoid certain activities or situations because they remind me of frightening experiences of the people I represent.

____24.   I am proud of what I can do to help.

____25.   As a result of my work, I have intrusive, frightening thoughts.

____26.   I feel 'bogged down' by the system.

____27.   I have thoughts that I am a 'success' as a lawyer.

____28.   I can't recall important parts of my work with trauma victims.

____29.   I am a very caring person.

____30.   I am happy that I chose to do this work.

Your scores on the ProQOL: professional quality of life screening

Based on your responses, place your personal scores below. If you have any concerns, you should discuss them with a physical or mental health care professional.

Compassion satisfaction_____

Compassion satisfaction is about the pleasure you derive from being able to do your work well. For example, you may feel like it is a pleasure to help others through your work. You may feel positively about your colleagues or your ability to contribute to the work setting or even the greater good of society. Higher scores on this scale represent a greater satisfaction related to your ability to be an effective caregiver in your job.

    If you are in the higher range, you probably derive a good deal of professional satisfaction from your position. If your scores are below 23, you may either find problems with your job, or there may be some other reason – for example, you might derive your satisfaction from activities other than your job. (Alpha scale reliability 0.88)

Burnout_____

Most people have an intuitive idea of what burnout is. From the research perspective, burnout is one of the elements of Compassion Fatigue (CF). It is associated with feelings of hopelessness and difficulties in dealing with work or in doing your job effectively. These negative feelings usually have a gradual onset. They can reflect the feeling that your efforts make no difference, or they can be associated with a very high workload or a non-supportive work environment. Higher scores on this scale mean that you are at higher risk for burnout.

If your score is below 23, this probably reflects positive feelings about your ability to be effective in your work. If you score above 41, you may wish to think about what at work makes you feel like you are not effective in your position. Your score may reflect your mood; perhaps you were having a 'bad day' or are in need of some time off. If the high score persists or if it is reflective of other worries, it may be a cause for concern. (Alpha scale reliability 0.75)

Secondary traumatic stress_____

The second component of Compassion Fatigue (CF) is secondary traumatic stress (STS). It is about your work related, secondary exposure to extremely or traumatically stressful events. Developing problems due to exposure to other's trauma is somewhat rare but does happen to many people who care for those who have experienced extremely or traumatically stressful events. For example, you may repeatedly hear stories about the traumatic things that happen to other people, commonly called Vicarious Traumatization. If your work puts you directly in the path of danger, for example, field work in a war or area of civil violence, this is not secondary exposure; your exposure is primary. However, if you are exposed to others' traumatic events as a result of your work, for example, as a therapist or an emergency worker, this is secondary exposure. The symptoms of STS are usually rapid in onset and associated with a particular event. They may include being afraid, having difficulty sleeping, having images of the upsetting event pop into your mind, or avoiding things that remind you of the event.

If your score is above 41, you may want to take some time to think about what at work may be frightening to you or if there is some other reason for the elevated score. While higher scores do not mean that you do have a problem, they are an indication that you may want to examine how you feel about your work and your work environment. You may wish to discuss this with your supervisor, a colleague, or a health care professional. (Alpha scale reliability 0.81)

What is my score and what does it mean?

In this section, you will score your test so you understand the interpretation for you. To find your score on **each section**, total the questions listed on the left and then find your score in the table on the right of the section.

Compassion satisfaction scale

Copy your rating on each of these questions on to this table and add them up. When you have added then up you can find your score on the table to the right.

Scores	The sum of my Compassion Satisfaction questions is	And my Compassion Satisfaction level is
3. ____	22 or less	Low
6. ____	Between 23 and 41	Moderate
12. ____		
16. ____		
18. ____		
20. ____		
22. ____		
24. ____	42 or more	High
27. ____		
30. ____		
Total: ____		

Burnout scale

On the burnout scale you will need to take an extra step. Starred items are 'reverse scored.' If you scored the item 1, write a 5 beside it. The reason we ask you to reverse the scores is because scientifically the measure works better when these questions are asked in a positive way though they can tell us more about their negative form. For example, question 1. 'I am happy' tells us more about the effects of helping when you are *not* happy so you reverse the score.

You Wrote	Change to
1	5
2	4
3	3
4	2
5	1

Scores	The sum of my Burnout Questions is	And my Burnout level is
*1. ____ = ____	22 or less	Low
*4. ____ = ____	Between 23 and 41	Moderate
8. ____		
10. ____		
*15. ____ = ____		
*17. ____ = ____	42 or more	High
19. ____		
21. ____		
26. ____		
*29. ____ = ____		
Total: ____		

Secondary Traumatic Stress Scale

Just like you did on Compassion Satisfaction, copy your rating on each of these questions on to this table and add them up. When you have added then up you can find your score on the table to the right.

Scores	The sum of my Secondary Trauma questions is	And my Secondary Traumatic Stress level is
2. ____	22 or less	Low
5. ____		
7. ____	Between 23 and 41	Moderate
9. ____		
11. ____		
13. ____		
14. ____		
23. ____	42 or more	High
25. ____		
28. ____		
Total: ____		

Further reading and resources

Some suggested texts and resources for further reading.

Books

Trauma

Judith Lewis Herman, *Trauma and Recovery*, Pandora, 1992

Staci K Haines, *The Politics of Trauma*, North Atlantic Books, 2019

Bessel van der Kolk, *The Body Keeps the Score: mind, brain, and body in the transformation of trauma*, Penguin, 2015

Resmaa Menakem, *My Grandmother's Hands*, Central Recovery Press, 2017

Stephen Regel and Stephen Joseph, *Post-traumatic Stress*, Oxford University Press, 2017

Vicarious trauma and compassion fatigue

Françoise Mathieu, *The Compassion Fatigue Workbook*, Routledge, 2012

Practical tools

David A Treleaven, *Trauma Sensitive Mindfulness*, WW Norton & Company, 2018

David Emerson and Elizabeth Hopper PhD, *Overcoming Trauma Through Yoga*, North Atlantic Books, 2011

Natalie Goldberg, *Writing Down the Bones*, Shambala Publications Inc, 2016

Mental health

Lisa Appignanesi, *Mad, Bad and Sad: A History of Women and the Mind Doctors from 1800 to the Present*, Virago, 2008

Nathan Filer, *This Book will Change Your Mind about Mental Health*, Faber & Faber 2019

Suman Fernando, *Mental Health, Race and Culture*, Red Globe Press, 2010

Articles and online resources

G Maguire and MK Byrne (2017), 'The law is not as blind as it seems: relative rates of vicarious trauma among lawyers and mental health professionals', *Psychiatry, Psychology and Law*, 24(2), 233–243. https://doi.org/10.1080/1321 8719.2016.1220037

Marie-Eve Leclerc, Jo-Anne Wemmers and Alain Brunet (2020), 'The unseen cost of justice: post-traumatic stress symptoms in Canadian lawyers', *Psychology, Crime & Law*, 26:1, 1-21, DOI: 10.1080/1068316X.2019.1611830

Line Rønning, Jocelyn Blumberg and Jesper Dammeyer (2020), 'Vicarious traumatisation in lawyers working with traumatised asylum seekers: a pilot study', *Psychiatry, Psychology and Law*, DOI: 10.1080/13218719.2020.1742238

PL Vrklevski and J Franklin (2008), 'Vicarious trauma: The impact on solicitors of exposure to traumatic material', *Traumatology*, 14(1), 106–118. https://doi.org/10.1177/1534765607309961

Online resources

The Advocate's Gateway
Free access to practical, evidence-based guidance on vulnerable witnesses and defendants: www.theadvocatesgateway.org

The Headington Institute
Not-for-profit team of psychologists in the USA that provides resources for frontline staff: www.headington-institute.org/resources/

Race Reflections
Offer, among many other resources, training on racial trauma: www.racereflections.co.uk

Suggested resources for the legal profession

All references correct at time of publication

Claiming Space
Facilitated peer support, bespoke training and consultancy
www.claiming.space

Family Law in Practice Faculty ('FLIP Faculty')
FLIP Faculty run a diploma course to train family law supervisors to provide one-to-one support for the sector
www.flipfaculty.org

Freedom from Torture
Training for immigration practitioners working with torture survivors
https://www.freedomfromtorture.org/help-for-survivors/
training-for-organisations

Immigration Law Practitioners' Association (ILPA)
https://ilpa.org.uk/members-area/working-groups/well-being-new/
well-being-resource-hub/
(ILPA also co-run the training with Freedom from Torture)

LawCare
The mental health charity for the legal profession in the UK and Ireland.
www.lawcare.org.uk
Helpline: 0800 279 6888

Law Society of Scotland
Resources and guidance on trauma-informed practice
https://www.lawscot.org.uk/members/cpd-training/online-cpd/
trauma-informed-training/

Wellbeing at the Bar
Resources and an Assistance Programme for members of all self-employed
barristers with a practicing certificate as well as member of the Institute of
Barristers' Clerks and the Legal Practice Managers' Association
https://www.wellbeingatthebar.org.uk

Index